Walt Whitman's

MEMORANDA DURING THE WAR

DEATH OF ABRAHAM LINCOLN

Lincoln's Picture <u>Keep Carefully</u>

one of the latest taken
before he was shot —
the most satisfactory
picture of A. L. I have
ever seen (and I have seen
hundreds of different ones) — Looks
just life I saw him last on the balcony
of the National Hotel

Feinberg Collection.

WALT WHITMAN'S

Memoranda During the War
[&] Death of Abraham Lincoln

reproduced in facsimile

———

EDITED WITH AN INTRODUCTION BY

ROY P. BASLER

1 9 6 2

Indiana University Press : Bloomington

CONTENTS

INTRODUCTION

Whitman's Record of the Civil War

AMONG the many diaries, reminiscences, and first-hand accounts of the Civil War written by those who experienced it, as citizens, soldiers, politicians, or whatever, Whitman's *Memoranda During the War* is unique, both for its particulars and for the deep sympathy and sharp perception with which the particulars are comprehended. With his customary aplomb he could describe it, even before it was fully written, as "an ardent book arresting the way of the most significant things . . . that characterize the time . . . full of the blood & vitality of the American people. . . ." Whitman had not merely the reporter's good eye for vivid details, but the poet's emotional involvement with those details. He recorded from the heart, in his prose as well as in his rhythmic jottings, trial lines for possible poems, which frequently appear in his diaries and hospital notebooks along with scraps of mere information—names and addresses, details of scene, items wanted by or given to the wounded. Certainly this was because Whitman was much of the time the poet as he went his rounds with his little home-made notebooks tied together with string, or pinned with a pin. But it is perhaps more that he was a sensitive, almost feminine, spirit, identifying himself personally with those individuals, places, and things which he observed. He was not merely concerned with gathering impressions, but also with giving an impression, careful to be clean, to present a cheerful and friendly manner, and to communicate himself, Walt Whitman, friend and companion.

What is mawkish or manly may be variously experienced by different persons, but the genuineness and profound humanity of Whitman's involvement with people is the unbroken scarlet thread woven through the entire fabric of this book no less than through the poems—in which human brotherhood is his central theme. It was given to no other, not even to Abraham Lincoln, to become more deeply involved in the human experience that was the Civil War, and in his own way Whitman gives us this experience more memorably than any other writer of the time, with the possible exception of Lincoln. It is this perhaps which has led to Whitman and Lincoln becoming the poles of an axis around which the poetic, which is to say the durable, meaning of the Civil War revolves. Between them and through them flows the whole field of magnetic experience recorded by other writers, politicians, soldiers, journalists, or everyday citizens. Lincoln at one pole was the embodiment of democracy in the public man as leader and statesman, and above all as the great captain. Whitman at the other pole was the embodiment of democracy in the private man as citizen and brother, and above all as the great poet.

Whitman played a personal role in no great events or decisions. He was just one drop of the "rolling ocean the crowd." But he was no merely passive spectator. His actions were those he found to do as one of the many, in his own way, not the least being to write down what he did, what he saw, what he thought and felt. In so doing he would enlarge himself, the bard of democracy and the poet of the "special event, incisive enough to mark with deepest cut, and mnemonize this turbulent Nineteenth century."

Whitman saw the possibilities of this binary relationship with Lincoln, perhaps not clearly at first, when so strongly drawn to admire the President, whom he confided in a diary note dated November 1, 1863, that he "loved personally," but surely and purposefully when, following the assassination, he set about writing the two most famous of his poems, "O Captain! My Captain!" and "When Lilacs Last in the Dooryard Bloom'd." To recognize that in later years Whitman unaertook to make the most of this relationship in no way derogates from either his sincerity or the special significance of his claim. It is given to poets to choose both their personal heroes and the matter of their songs, and had Whitman been less a poet he might have been more reluctant to risk the jealousy of others who would claim Lincoln in some way as their personal prerogative. When he came in later years to the compilation of *Memoranda During the War* and the preparation of his lecture "Death of Abraham Lincoln," the relationship was so strongly established in Whitman's mind that he had to be on guard against letting his emotional attachment to Lincoln run away with the facts as he recollected them.

A fragment of manuscript, preserved in the Harned Collection in the Library of Congress, which appears to have been discarded from one or another of Whitman's published Lincoln pieces, illustrates this danger:

But the time speeds—soon a few only—in a few years only a few scores here and there of the veterans of those times will remain.

What a precious interest there will soon attach to every incident, especially of Abraham Lincoln. What a thrill will —what a solemnity will fall upon all, run through a crowd of listeners—or the children and young people at some such old centenarian's answer "Yes I saw him, he spoke to me— I touched his hands, I heard his voice."—I was one of those who

Holograph fragment of an essay on Lincoln.
Harned Collection, Library of Congress.

There the scrap ends, and through the last, incomplete sentence, ''I was one of those who'' a strong line is drawn, cancelling the temptation to slip into factual untruth on the wave of imagination.

Whitman saw Lincoln frequently during the years 1863–65 and wrote of his admiration and affection for the President in letters and diary notes, but nowhere is there any evidence that he ever met or shook hands with the man whom he later acknowledged to be ''particularly my man.''

W. E. Barton's statement in *Abraham Lincoln and Walt Whitman* (1928) that Whitman wrote ''no single line of praise while Lincoln was living, and wrote no testimony of any sort of his affection for the great President,'' is, as are many of the statements in this biased book, patently false. Whitman wrote his friend J. P. Kirkwood in March, 1863:

I see the President often. I think better of him than many do. He has conscience and homely shrewdness—conceals an enormous tenacity under his mild gawky western manner. The difficulties of his situation have been unprecedented in the history of statesmanship. That he has conserved the government so far is a miracle. . . . [Original owned by Charles E. Feinberg]

Again on March 19, 1863, he wrote his friends Nat and Fred Gray:

I think well of the President. He has a face like a Hoosier Michael Angelo, so awful ugly it becomes beautiful, with its strange mouth, its deep cut, criss-cross lines, and its doughnut complexion. My notion is too, that underneath his outside smutched mannerism, and stories from third-class county bar-rooms, (it is his humor,) Mr. Lincoln keeps a fountain of first-class practical telling wisdom. I do not dwell on the supposed failures of his government; he has shown, I sometimes think an almost supernatural tact in keeping the ship afloat at all, with head steady, not only not going down, and now certain not to, but with proud and resolute spirit, and flag flying in sight of the world, menacing and high as ever. I say never yet captain, never ruler, had such a perplexing dangerous task as his, the past two years. I more and more rely upon his idiomatic western genius, careless of court dress or court decorums. [Original in the Clifton Waller Barrett Collection, Alderman Library, University of Virginia]

Again on June 30, 1863, he wrote to his mother:

Mr. Lincoln passes here (14th st.) every evening about half-past 6—he was in his barouche, two horses, guarded by about thirty cavalry. The barouche comes first under a slow trot, driven by one man in the box, no servant or footman beside; the cavalry all follow closely after with a lieutenant at their head. I had a good view of the President last evening. He looks more careworn even than usual, his face with deep cut lines, seams, and his *complexion gray* through very dark skin—a curious looking man, very sad. I said to a lady who was looking with me, "Who can see that man without losing all wish to be sharp upon him personally?" The lady assented, although she is almost vindictive on the course of the administration (thinks it wants nerve, etc.—the usual complaint). The equipage is rather shabby, horses indeed almost what my friends the Broadway drivers would call *old plugs*. The President dresses in plain black clothes, cylinder hat—he was alone yesterday. As he came up, he first drove over to the house of the Sec. of War, on K st., about 300 feet from here; sat in his carriage while Stanton came out and had a 15 minutes interview with him (I can see from my window), and then wheeled around the corner and up Fourteenth st., the cavalry after him. I really think it would be safer for him just now to stop at the White

House, but I expect he is too proud to abandon the former custom. [*The Wound Dresser* (1898), pp. 90–91]

Other letters, such as one to Mrs. Abby Price, October 11, 1863, or the one to his mother, April 26, 1864, in a similar vein of affection, trust, and praise, demolish Barton's thesis so effectively that one wonders how, when the letters to Whitman's mother were available in print, as were the memorable passages from the notebooks published in *Memoranda,* even Barton's obvious dislike for Whitman could have so misled him. Perhaps the answer lies in the truth which Barton perceived, as anyone may—that Whitman grew to be more and more popularly identified with Lincoln in after years, and as a result came himself to think of Lincoln as in some fashion peculiarly his man. It is too bad that Barton, who was in his own way motivated by a similar impulse, as attested by more books about Lincoln than any other writer has produced, could not allow room for Whitman's great affection.

Whitman's account of his ministrations to sick and wounded soldiers as given so vividly in *Memoranda During the War* is supplemented in his letters, most notably those included in *The Wound Dresser* (1898), and has been treated at length by various biographers. One incident of the story which has not been clearly understood, however, may receive brief comment—his connection with the Christian Commission.

This organization had been formed by the churches to carry on much the same kind of activities that were performed in World Wars I and II by the Red Cross and similar organizations. Sometime after his

No. *158*

Office Christian Commission,

No. 13 Bank Street.

Philadelphia, Jany 20th 1863

To Officers of the Army and Navy of the United States, and others:

The **CHRISTIAN COMMISSION,** organized by a Convention of the Young Men's Christian Associations of the loyal States, to promote the spiritual and temporal welfare and improvement of the men of the Army and Navy, acting under the approbation and commendation of the President, the Secretaries of the Army and the Navy, and of the Generals in command, have appointed

Walt Whitman of Brooklyn N.Y.

A Delegate, to act in accordance with instructions furnished herewith, under direction of the proper officers, in furtherance of the objects of the Christian Commission.

His services will be rendered in behalf of the Christian Commission, without remuneration from, or expense to, the Government.

His work will be that of distributing stores where needed, in hospitals and camps; circulating good reading matter amongst soldiers and sailors; visiting the sick and wounded, to instruct, comfort and cheer them, and aid them in correspondence with their friends at home; aiding Surgeons on the battle-field and elsewhere in the care and conveyance of the wounded to hospitals; helping Chaplains in their ministrations and influence for the good of the men under their care; and addressing soldiers and sailors, individually and collectively, in explanation of the work of the Christian Commission and its Delegates, and for their personal instruction and benefit, temporal and eternal.

All possible facilities, and all due courtesies, are asked for him, in the proper pursuance of any or all of these duties.

Geo. H. Stuart

Chairman Christian Commission.

Whitman's credentials as a Christian Commission delegate.
Feinberg Collection.

Christian Commission,

Office, 13 Bank Street, Philadelphia.

GEO. H. STUART, Esq., *Chairman*, 13 *Bank St.*   JOS. PATTERSON, Esq., *Treasurer, Western Bank.*
REV. W. E. BOARDMAN, *Secretary*, 13 *Bank St.*

MEMBERS OF THE CHRISTIAN COMMISSION.

REV. ROLLIN H. NEALE, D. D., *Boston.*
CHARLES DEMOND, Esq., *Boston.*
REV. BISHOP E. S. JANES, D. D., *New York.*
REV. JAMES EELLS, D. D., *Brooklyn.*
MITCHELL H. MILLER, Esq., *Washington.*
GEO. H. STUART, Esq., *Philadelphia.*

JOHN P. CROZER, Esq., *Philadelphia.*
JAY COOKE, Esq., *Philadelphia.*
REV. M. L. R. P. THOMPSON, D. D., *Cincinnati.*
COL. CLINTON B. FISK, *St. Louis.*
JOHN V. FARWELL, Esq., *Chicago.*
JOHN D. HILL, M. D., *Buffalo.*

The accompanying Letters are gratifying evidences that the Government cordially approves our plan, and will aid us so far as it lawfully may:

Letter from President Lincoln.

EXECUTIVE MANSION,
WASHINGTON, *December* 12, 1861.

My Dear Sir—Your letter of the 11th inst. and accompanying plan, both of which are returned as a convenient mode of connecting this with them, have just been received. Your Christian and benevolent undertaking for the benefit of the soldiers, is too obviously proper and praiseworthy to admit any difference of opinion. I sincerely hope your plan may be as successful in execution as it is just and generous in conception.

Your obedient servant,

GEO. H. STUART, ESQ.,   A. LINCOLN.
Chairman "Christian Commission," Philadelphia, Pa.

Letter from the Secretary of War.

WAR DEPARTMENT, *December* 13, 1861.

Sir—This Department approves the object of the "CHRISTIAN COMMISSION," as set forth in the circular announcing their appointment by a convention of the delegates of the Young Men's Christian Associations, held in the City of New York, Nov. 14th and 15th, 1861.

This Department is deeply interested in the "spiritual good of the soldiers in our army," as well as in their "intellectual improvement, and social and physical comfort," and will cheerfully give its aid to the benevolent and patriotic of the land, who desire to improve the condition of our troops.

It confidently looks for beneficial results from so noble an enterprise, and begs you to express to the Commission its sincere wish for the success of this great work in behalf of the soldier.

Very respectfully, your obedient servant,

SIMON CAMERON, *Secretary of War.*

GEO. H. STUART, ESQ.,
Chairman "Christian Commission," Philadelphia, Pa.

Letter from the Secretary of the Navy.

NAVY DEPARTMENT, *December* 16, 1861.

Sir—I have received your letter of the 11th inst., asking an expression of the Department as to the objects of the "CHRISTIAN COMMISSION," to promote the welfare of the soldiers, sailors, marines, &c.

The Department will be gratified with any legitimate means to promote the welfare (present and future) of all who are in the service.

I am, very respectfully,

Your obedient servant,

Mr. GEO. H. STUART,   GIDEON WELLES.
Chairman Christian Commission,
Philadelphia.

Letter from Gen. McClellan.

HEAD QUARTERS, ARMY OF THE POTOMAC,
Washington, June 8, 1861.

GEO. H. STUART, ESQ., *Philadelphia.*

Dear Sir—I have the honor to acknowledge the receipt of your letter, informing me of the appointment by the Convention of the Young Men's Christian Association, of a Commission to take active measures to promote the spiritual and temporal welfare of our soldiers and sailors.

The objects of the Commission are such as meet my cordial approval, and will, if carried out in the proper spirit, prove of great value.

Very respectfully,

Your obedient servant,

GEO. B. McCLELLAN.

The Christian Commission: Officers and testimonial letters.
Feinberg Collection.

arrival in Washington on December 17, 1862, Whitman apparently applied to the Christian Commission as a volunteer, and on January 20, 1863, a commission was issued, signed by George H. Stuart, Chairman, Christian Commission. The original commission in the collection of Charles E. Feinberg, reproduced in facsimile herewith, should leave no question of the fact which has been repeatedly doubted or denied by Whitman's biographers.

Although Whitman seems not to have referred specifically to his own connection with the Christian Commission, he wrote his mother on June 22, 1863, that unlike the Sanitary Commissioners, whom he thought "incompetent and disagreeable; as I told you before, the only good fellows I have met are the Christian commissioners—they go everywhere and receive no pay." In fact, it may be supposed that, if not entirely a requisite to his own entree to the hospital wards, his commission ˙must certainly have been the passport which facilitated his continual visits.

Publication of Memoranda During the War

MEMORANDA DURING THE WAR is one of the rarer pieces of Whitmaniana. Only thirty-two copies have been located by the present writer, and Whitman bibliographer Carolyn Wells estimated (*A Concise Bibliography of the Works of Walt Whitman*, 1922) that less than a hundred copies were ever printed.

Whitman's interest in publishing a volume composed of excerpts from his war diaries and hospital notebooks began to take form in 1863. On October 21 of that year he wrote to his friend James Redpath, the Boston publisher and biographer of John Brown (1860), proposing a book to be entitled ''Memoranda of a Year'':

My idea is a book of the time, worthy the time,—something considerably beyond mere hospital sketches—a book for sale perhaps in a larger American market—the premises or skeleton memoranda of incidents, persons, places, sights, the past year (mostly jotted down either on the spot or in the spirit of seeing or hearing what is narrated (I left New York early last December and have been around in the front or here ever since)—full of interest I surely think—in some respects somewhat a combination in handling of the old French Memoires & my own personality (things seen through my eyes & what my vision brings)—a book full enough of mosaic but all fused to one comprehensive theory —one of the main drifts is to push forward the very big & needed truth that our National military system needs shifting, revolutionizing & made to tally with democracy, the people. The officers should almost invariably rise from the ranks—the entire capacity, keenness & courage of our army are in the ranks—there is an absolute want of democratic spirit in the present system & officers—it is the feudal spirit exclusively. What has been done has been unavoidable so far, but the time has arrived to discuss the charge.

I have much to say of the hospitals, the immense national hospitals—significant incidents, persons &c—in them too most radical changes of premises are demanded—(The air the spirit of a thing is everything, the details follow and adjust themselves). . . .

I have many hospital incidents that will take with the general reader—I ventilate my general democracy with details very largely,—& with reference to the future—bring in persons, the President, Seward, Congress, the Capitol, Washington City, many of the actors of the drama—have something to say of the great trunk America, the West &c &c—do not hesitate to diffuse *myself*. . . . [Original draft, Van Sinderen Collection, Yale University]

Whitman's enthusiasm carried him to the point of blocking out the title page and the publisher's prospectus shown here in facsimile, but Redpath replied on October 28:

Friend W.

I have taken your proposition into consideration.

There is a lion in the way—$

I could easily publish a small Book, but the one you propose—to stereotype, advertise and push it—implies an expenditure that may be beyond my means. But if I can get credit, I may try. Whether I will or no depends somewhat on the printer's notions as to whether the book would sell.

Suppose you finish it and send it on: if I can't publish it, I will see if some other person won't.

This is the best I can safely promise you. If I can get one or two jobbers to read and like it, and they will make an advance order, or give a favorable trade opinion, the way is clear. . . . [Traubel, *With Walt Whitman in Camden*, 1953, IV, 418]

Whitman's title page for his proposed book.
Van Sinderen Collection, Yale University Library.

Walt Whitman's [Publishers announcement]

A New Book

by walt whitman

Memoranda of a year

Probably no greater year has ever sped to its close, in the world's history, than the one now about terminated. At all events it is the most important in the history of America. And this book, jotted down on the battle field in the shelter tent, on by the war side amid passing artillery trains, or the mass of cavalry, in the gorgeous halls of gold, where the national representatives meet, and above all in the great military hospitals, among the blood, the ashy face, the bloody bandage, with death & suffering on every side

Part of Whitman's prospectus for his proposed book.
Van Sinderen Collection, Yale University Library.

Whitman's conclusion to his prospectus.
Van Sinderen Collection, Yale University Library.

Nothing further seems to have come of this proposal for the time being, but Whitman did not abandon the idea. From time to time events brought to his mind the possibility of composing a narrative of the war, prose or poem. Such an incident occurred on the day after Christmas, 1864, when his brother George's trunk arrived at his mother's home, where Walt was spending the holidays. His diary entry for December 26 records the event.

Monday night. December 26, 1864.—I am writing this in the front basement in Portland avenue, Brooklyn, at home.) It is after 9 o'clock at night. We have had a wet day with fog, mud, slush, & the yet unmelted hard-polished ice liberally left in the streets. All sluggish & damp, with a prevailing leaden vapor. Yesterday, Christmas, about the same. (George's trunk came by express to-day, early in forenoon, from City Point, Virginia. Lt. Babcock, of the 51st was kind enough to search it out there & send it home. It stood some hours before we felt inclined to open it. Towards evening mother & Eddy looked over the things. One could not help feeling depressed. There were his uniform coat, pants, sash, &c. There were many things reminded us of him. Papers, memoranda, books, nick-nacks, a revolver, a small diary, roll of his company, a case of photographs of his comrades (several of them I knew as killed in battle,) with other stuff such as a soldier accumulates. Mother looked every thing over, laid out the shirts to be washed, the coats & pants to hang up, & all the rest were carefully put back. It made us feel pretty solemn. We have not heard from him since October 3d; whether living or dead we know not. I am aware of the condition of the union prisoners south, through seeing them, when brought up & from lately talking with a friend just returned from taking part in the exchange at Savannah & Charleston by which we have received 12,000 of our sick. Their situation, as of all our men in prison, is indescribably horrible. Hard, ghastly starvation is the rule.

Rags, filth, despair, in large open stockades, no shelter, no cooking, no clothes,—such the condition of masses of men, in some places two or three thousand, & in the largest prison as high as thirty thousand confined. The guards are insufficient in numbers, & they make it up by treble severity, shooting the prisoners literally just to keep them under terrorism. I cannot get any reliable trace of the 51st officers at all. I supposed they were at Columbia, South Carolina, but my friend has brought a list purporting to be complete record of all in confinement there, & I cannot find any of the 51st among them.

To night I have been looking over Georges diary. It comes down to about the 1st of September 1863. It is merely a skeleton of dates, voyages, places camped in or marched through, battles fought, &c. But I can realize clearly that by calling upon even a tithe of the myriads of living & actual facts, which go along with, & fill up this dry list of times & places, it would outvie all the romances in the world, & most of the famous histories & biographies to boot. It does not need calling in play the imagination to see that in such a record as this lies folded a perfect poem of the war comprehending all its phases, its passions, the fierce tug of the secessionists, the interminable fibre of the national union, all the special hues & characteristic forms & pictures of the actual battles with colors flying, rifles snapping, cannon thundering, grape whirring, armies struggling, ships at sea or bombarding shore batteries, skirmishes in woods, great pitched battles, & all the profound scenes of individual death, courage, endurance & superbest hardihood, & splendid muscular, wrestle of a newer larger race of human giants with all furious passions aroused on one side, & the sternness of an unalterable determination on the other. [Original in the Van Sinderen Collection, Yale University]

Nearly a decade later, in January, 1874, he began publishing in the *Weekly Graphic* a series of six articles entitled " 'Tis But Ten Years Since," the first of which appeared on January 29 and the last on March 7. On February 27, 1874, Whitman wrote to President Grant:

> . . . I take the liberty of sending (same mail with this) some reminiscences I have written about the war, in Nos. of the N. Y. Weekly Graphic, and thinking you of all men can best return to them in the vein in which they are composed.
>
> I am not sure whether you will remember me—or my occasional salute to you in Washington! I am laid up here with tedious paralysis but think I shall get well & return to Washington. . . .

Whitman received a reply from President Grant's secretary Levi P. Luckey, dated March 6, 1874:

> The President desires me to acknowledge the receipt of your very kind letter of the 27th ultimo, also the numbers of the N. Y. Weekly Graphic, containing your reminiscences of the war.
>
> He wishes me to assure you of his appreciation of the polite attention, and of his best wishes for your speedy recovery. [Original owned by Charles E. Feinberg]

These *Weekly Graphic* articles were largely composed of what seem to be many of the same excerpts from his diaries and notebooks which were incorporated the following year, 1875, with minor deletions and major additions, in *Memoranda During the War*. (See T. O. Mabbott and R. G. Silver, " 'Tis But Ten Years Since," *American Literature*, XV, 51–62, March, 1943, for a reprinting of the few insignificant passages which do not appear in Whitman's later works.) These articles also drew on another piece which Whitman composed about this time entitled ''The Centennial,'' on the first page of which appears

Whitman's note, "Much of this is used in ' 'Tis But 10 Years Since' " (original owned by Charles E. Feinberg).

Although the "memoranda" seem obviously to have been, as Whitman described them to Redpath, "jotted down either on the spot or in the spirit of seeing and hearing what is narrated," it is not easy to verify what was copied verbatim from the diaries and notebooks and what was written out from memory later. Relatively few verbatim passages have been discovered in any of the numerous manuscript notebooks and diaries seen by the present writer. As in the case of Whitman's poems, final manuscripts which served as the original printer's copy seem to be relatively rare, perhaps to some extent because of Whitman's practice of getting the thing set in type at an early stage, and thereafter furnishing revised proofs instead of manuscript to the newspapers, periodicals, or book publishers that would first present the piece to the public. Early drafts and revisions in manuscript are far more common than final manuscript in the Whitman collections known to the present writer. Three examples which correspond to passages on pages 3, 46, and 48 of *Memoranda During the War,* shown here in facsimile, are obviously neither original diary pages nor verbatim copies, but rather drafts, perhaps "written out from memory" in January, 1874. The fourth example seems to be an original diary page with only a portion of the item as it appears, revised and expanded on page 9 in *Memoranda During the War.*

On January 16, 1874, Whitman wrote his friend Peter Doyle, "If you come across the *Weekly Graphic* just out get it, as I have commenced a series of pieces

in life, more years, 6
visit the sick & wounded of
the Army, both on the field
& in the Hospitals of Washington city & its adjacencies. I
found it necessary to keep
little note-books, merely sheets
of paper, folded, to carry handily
in the pocket — for cases, names,
incidents &c. It is to these
Memoranda, briefly & rapidly
pencilled on the spot that I
transcribe quite all the following
incidents. Whatever they do not
have, they have at least the
qualities of being written amid the scenes,
spot & of presenting what the eyes
saw and the heart felt at the
time, perhaps out of conveying the
more or less, the convulsive temper
and

Holograph draft of *Memoranda During the War*, page 3.
Henry E. Huntington Library.

Holograph draft of *Memoranda During the War*, page 46.
Harned Collection, Library of Congress.

Holograph draft of *Memoranda During the War*, page 48.
Harned Collection, Library of Congress.

Holograph note, expanded in *Memoranda During the War*,
page 9. *Henry E. Huntington Library.*

about things just before and during the war.'' (*The
Complete Prose Works*, G. P. Putnam's Sons, New
York and London, 1902, V, 131.) This seems to be
Whitman's first reference to the ''memoranda'' since
his letter to Redpath, October 21, 1863.

Of course, Whitman was not an eyewitness of every
incident or scene which he included in *Memoranda
During the War*. For the writing of those he did not
witness, he went about collecting his material just
as any good reporter or historian would. Many clippings and scraps of manuscript notes preserved in
various collections of Whitmaniana testify to this
preliminary work, such as those in the Harned Collection: ''The Doctor's statement going into battle''
(December, 1862), ''Scene in the woods on the Peninsula told me by Milton Roberts,'' or ''Punishment
of Soldiers—Lewis K. Brown'' (Nos. 94, 101, and 99
in *Walt Whitman, A Catalog*, The Library of Congress, Washington, 1955). The most famous episode,
Lincoln's death, was carefully researched, for Whit-

man was in Brooklyn when it occurred, as he re-called in later years: "The day of the murder we heard the news very early in the morning. Mother prepared breakfast—and other meals afterward—as usual; but not a mouthful was eaten all day by either of us. We each drank half a cup of coffee; that was all. Little was said. We got every newspaper morning and evening, and the frequent extras of that period, and pass'd them silently to each other." (*The Complete Writings of Walt Whitman,* 1902, IV, 37–38.)

Nevertheless, when Whitman wrote the episode of April 14, 1865, for *Memoranda During the War,* he undertook to give it the effect of an eyewitness account.

Aside from the consistent drive to publish, at his own expense and in spite of terrific obstacles, the stimulus which prompted the eventual preparation and publication of *Memoranda During the War* was obviously Whitman's wish to provide posterity with an autobiographical memento in the face of possible and, as it seemed at the time, even imminent death. On February 3, 1874, at the time when Whitman was preparing the series of articles for the *Weekly Graphic,* he wrote the wife of his friend William Douglas O'Connor, "Nelly Death has become to me a familiar thing—yet, as I sit here writing, I do not feel a particle less of life in me, than ever" (Allen, *The Solitary Singer,* p. 456). On February 11, writing her again, he indicated the extremity of his dejection, "I have twice hurriedly destroyed a large mass of letters & MSS.—to be ready for what might happen" (*ibid.*).

From the date of his first paralytic stroke on January 23, 1873, until April, 1876, when *Memoranda*

During the War was finally in press, Whitman was
never very far from the thought and even the ex-
pectancy of death. Two elegiac poems composed during the same period as the articles for the *Weekly
Graphic*, "Song of the Redwood Tree" and "Prayer
of Columbus" were symbolically autobiographical of
his waning strength and awareness of death. Of
"Prayer of Columbus," he wrote Ellen O'Connor, "I
shouldn't wonder if I have unconsciously put a sort
of autobiographical dash in it" (*ibid.*, 458). Likewise,
the epigraph chosen for the volume of poems and
prose *Two Rivulets*, which was also published in 1876,
suggested that Whitman recognized the possibility
that this might well be his last book. The lines were
taken from the poem which gave the volume its title,
"Two Rivulets":

For the Eternal Ocean bound,
These ripples, passing surges, streams of Death and Life.

Two Rivulets was compiled as the second volume of
the "Centennial Edition" of Whitman's works, to be
issued in 1876 in connection with the Centennial Ex-
position at Philadelphia, *Leaves of Grass* being the
first. In this volume Whitman arranged new material,
such as *Memoranda During the War*, along with previously printed separates in what has been described
as "quite a hodgepodge" (Allen, 463), with each
section paginated separately and with a somewhat
confusing table of contents. The character of the
volume arises both from Whitman's necessary econ-
omy in using stereotype plates of the previously
printed separates and from his intention to issue
some, at least, of the new pieces also as separates,
notably *Memoranda During the War*. *Two Rivulets*

is composed as follows: (1) "Two Rivulets" (1876) 32 pages; (2) "Democratic Vistas" (c. 1870) 84 pages; (3) "Centennial Songs" (c. 1875) 18 pages; (4) "As a Strong Bird on Pinions Free and Other Poems" (c. 1872) 14 numbered pages plus 2 unnumbered pages containing "Virginia—the West" and "By Broad Potomac Shores"; (5) "Memoranda During the War" (1875–'76) beginning with the title page and without the preliminary pages of the separate printing, 68 pages; (6) "Passage to India" (c. 1870) 120 pages; (7) advertisement for *Memoranda During the War* "by itself, separate, in one thin Volume, 68 pages, 12 mo., neatly bound. . . . Price $1.50."

For the separate printing of *Memoranda During the War* Whitman added the pages preceding the title page as reproduced in the present volume. Among extant copies, however, there are some which do not bear these preliminary pages. These are, as in the case of one preserved in the Library of Congress, apparently proof sheets bound in after years as separates by Horace Traubel, or someone else. The copy in the Library of Congress bears an inscription by Traubel dated 1905, "from a mass of printed refuse given by Walt Whitman to me to be thrown away. I put the sheets in trim to Percival Wiksell."

Lecture: "Death of Abraham Lincoln"

ALTHOUGH *Memoranda During the War* could not have been widely read in the separate printing, in its place among the pages of *Two Rivulets* as well perhaps as in the portions appearing in the series of articles printed in the *Weekly Graphic,* Whitman's description of the death of Abraham Lincoln became known. In addition, on February 12, 1876, the *New York Sun* reprinted the paragraphs from *Memoranda During the War* dated April 14, 1865, giving the story the title "Death of Lincoln." Two years later, on February 3, Whitman's friend the naturalist John Burroughs wrote that Richard Watson Gilder, editor of *Scribner's Monthly,* had suggested the possibility of Whitman's coming to New York to give a lecture on Lincoln (original in the Lion Collection, New York Public Library). Whitman replied on February 24, 1878:

I am agreeable to the Lecture project—if it can be put through—about the middle of April (the anniversary of the eve or night of Lincoln's murder) might be a good night— Everything would depend on how it was fixed up and prepared for & put through—Let me hear more particulars—I could be ready to splurge April 14th or 15th.—I am well, considering—in good flesh, appetite and trim generally. . . . [Original in the Doheny Collection, St. John's Seminary, Camarillo, California)

Burroughs replied immediately, on February 25:

I have done nothing & said nothing about the lecture since I wrote you, as hearing from you was the first thing in order. I think we can work the thing up by April. I shall go to N. Y. the last of this week & talk the matter up with

Gilder & [Edmund Clarence] Stedman & others. I know all depends upon how the matter is put through & we have time enough to go to work in order. I presume I shall go to N. Y. on Thursday: if you want to write me there, write care of Scribner's & Co. 743 Broadway. The 14th of April comes on Sunday. Monday night would be our time. . . . [Original owned by Charles E. Feinberg]

Burroughs and friends proceeded with the necessary arrangements, and Whitman began to prepare his lecture. The nucleus was at hand in the April 14 passage which the *New York Sun* had reprinted from *Memoranda During the War* (pages 46–49). This Whitman clipped out to become paragraphs 16 through 23 of the lecture. Another passage in *Memoranda During the War* (the note on pages 22–23), beginning "I shall not easily forget the first time I saw Abraham Lincoln," Whitman considerably revised and expanded to form paragraphs 6 through 10 of his lecture. Between these two excerpts from *Memoranda* he bridged what seems to be a mostly new passage to form paragraphs 11 through 15—new, that is, with the exception of a few lines of the thirteenth paragraph, which are identical with lines 22–29 on page 4 of *Memoranda*. To this main body he added the conclusion, also apparently new paragraphs, beginning with paragraph 24, "Thus the visible incidents . . ." continuing to the end of the lecture, and likewise the introductory paragraphs 2 through 5. Perhaps he did not complete all of his work until later, for during the month of March he suffered a setback in health and plans for the lecture were abandoned.

Whitman's recovery from the paralytic stroke suffered in 1873 had been at best very slow, but beginning in the summer of 1875, shortly after *Memoranda During the War* was put in press, he began to walk again. Although three years later he still walked with a dragging left foot, both he and his friends had come to think that he was, as he phrased it "well, considering—in good flesh, appetite and trim generally." But this temporary relapse, which lasted until the summer, prevented his giving the lecture as scheduled on April 15, 1878.

A year later, on the night of April 14 at Steck Hall in New York, Whitman first delivered his lecture. The *New York Tribune* for April 15 printed the entire lecture and described Whitman as reading "from notes, sitting in a chair, as he is still much disabled from paralysis." The *New York Sun* of the same date gave less space to the actual lecture but more to the occasion. According to the *Sun* the audience numbered "threescore or perhaps fourscore," Whitman "read his essay (which has long been published) in a conversational tone,'' and at the conclusion "read them the piece . . . 'Captain, oh, My Captain [*sic*]. . . .' ''

From these two accounts it may be inferred that Whitman read in part from a manuscript (the "notes" referred to by the *Tribune*) and in part from a printed text, *Memoranda During the War*, which the *Sun* reporter knew had been published for more than three years because the *Sun* had reprinted the April 14 episode as its Lincoln's birthday article on February 12, 1876.

The text of the lecture as printed in the *Tribune*, presumably from Whitman's manuscript, became the basic text, clippings from which Whitman worked the next year, 1880, in preparing to deliver the lec-

ture a second time, on April 15, at Association Hall,
Philadelphia. For this second lecture Whitman wrote
an additional introductory paragraph, which he had
set in type with full headlines and used together with
the text clipped from the *New York Tribune* to send
to newspapers in Camden, Philadelphia, and other
cities, in advance of the date, in order to obtain as
wide distribution of the lecture as possible. Shown in
facsimile is the example of this paragraph, which is
preserved in the Harned Collection in the Library of
Congress together with the first paragraph of the
body of the lecture which Whitman clipped from the
New York Tribune. The *Camden Daily Post* and the
Philadelphia Press for April 16 carried the lecture
substantially as Whitman had submitted it, but with
a few minor omissions. The *Press* reporter's introductory description reads as follows:

The audience that gathered in Association Hall to listen
to the 'Good Gray Poet's' reminiscences of Abraham Lincoln was one of which Mr. Whitman may well be proud;
not that it was so large, because more could have been ac-
commodated, but on account of the intelligence and re-
spectability of the assemblage. Not a few heads were as
snowy as that of the lecturer. A great many ladies were
present, and the showy colors that fashion warrants for
spring wear stood out very conspicuously. Mr. Whitman occupied the platform alone, and needed no introduction. An
outburst of applause greeted him as he walked haltingly
across the stage, and stood beside the desk. His method of
delivery was wholly devoid of tricks of elocution, the sen-
tences being uttered in a tone only sufficiently higher than
he would make use of in talking to a friend to make sure
that the most distant hearer would catch every word. Occasionally, in speaking of his personal affection for emancipation's martyr, his voice trembled and the eyes of not a

WALT WHITMAN LAST NIGHT

April 15. 1880. at Association Hall. Philadelphia

How often since that dark and dripping Saturday—that chilly April day, now fifteen years bygone—my heart has entertain'd the dream, the wish, to give of Abraham Lincoln's death its own special thought and memorial. Yet now the sought-for opportunity offers, I find my notes incompetent, (why, for truly profound themes, is statement so idle? why does the right phrase never offer?) and the fit tribute I dreamed of waits unprepared as ever. My talk here indeed is less because of itself or anything in it, and nearly altogether because I feel a desire, apart from any talk, to specify the day, the martyrdom. It is for this, my friends, I have called you together. Oft as the rolling years bring back this hour, let it again however briefly be dwelt upon. For my own part, I hope and intend, till my own dying day, whenever the 14th or 15th of April comes, to annually gather a few friends, and hold its tragic reminiscence. No narrow or sectional reminiscence. It belongs to These States in their entirety—not the North only, but the South—perhaps belongs most tenderly and devoutly to the South, of all; for there, really, this man's birth-stock. There and thence his antecedent stamp. Why should I not say that thence his manliest traits—his universality—his canny, easy ways and words upon the surface—his inflexible determination and courage at heart? Have you never realized it, my friends, that Lincoln, though grafted on the West, is essentially, in personnel and character, a Southern contribution?

To Brinton Don't mind the different type

Though by no means proposing to resume the Secession War to-night, I would briefly remind you, unreformed, of the public conditions preceding that contest. For twenty years, and especially during the four or five before the war actually began, the aspect of affairs in the United States, though without the flush of military excitement, presents more than the survey of a battle, or any extended campaign, or series, even of Nature's convulsions. The hot passions of the South—the strange mixture at the North of inertia, incredulity, and conscious power—the insanlarium of the Abolitionists—the rascality and grip of the politicians, unparalleled in any land, any age. To these I must not omit adding the honesty of the essential bulk of the people everywhere—yet with all the seething fury and contradiction of their natures more aroused than the Atlantic's waves in wildest equinox.

What could be more ominous (though generally unappreciated then)—what more significant than the Presidency of Fillmore and Buchanan? proving conclusively that the weakness and wickedness of elected rulers, backed by our great parties, are just as likely to affect us here, as in the countries of the Old World, under their monarchies, emperors and aristocracies. In that Old World were everywhere heard underground rumblings, that died out, only again surely to return. While in America the volcano, though civic yet, continued to grow more and more convulsive—more and more stormy and threatening.

In the height of all this excitement and chaos, hovering on the edge at first, and then merged in its very midst, and destined to play a leading part, appears a strange and awkward figure.

Whitman's new introduction to his second lecture, Philadelphia, April 15, 1880. *Harned Collection, Library of Congress.*

Ticket to Whitman's lecture, Philadelphia, April 15, 1880, and Whitman's list of persons sent complimentary tickets and copies of the *Camden Daily Post. Feinberg Collection.*

few of his hearers were tearful. He was frequently applauded, and after the lecture by request repeated his well-known poem on the same subject.

At about the same time, perhaps before or perhaps after the Association Hall lecture, Whitman had both the beginning of the lecture and the conclusion—all of it that is, except the April 14 section clipped from *Memoranda During the War*—set in type, from which several proofs were taken. Perhaps he intended, or considered the possibility of, printing it separately as a pamphlet. In any event, these proofs, together with the clipping from *Memoranda*, became from this point onward the basic text of the lecture. Whitman used them to mark up as the printer's copy for the piece as it was included in *Specimen Days and Collect* (1882). This set as well as another unmarked set is in the Feinberg Collection. In addition, Whitman used a set of these proofs to prepare the "pocketbook" reading copy which he used when reading his lecture in following years. This reading copy was given by Horace Traubel to Robert G. Ingersoll, and is now also in the Feinberg Collection. With its text much revised as the lecture was repeated year after year, this copy is reproduced in facsimile in the present volume on the pages following *Memoranda During the War*, as a worthy companion piece in its own right, but especially for Whitman's numerous autograph revisions and insertions which add to the basic text as printed in *Specimen Days and Collect* and reproduced in later editions of Whitman's works.

Whitman made this pocket-size reading book by cutting down a copy of a novel published in 1878, *The Bride of Gettysburg* by John Dunbar Hylton.

He pasted the end papers of the book together, pasted yellow glazed paper over the covers, then cut and pasted the lecture proof sheets to succeeding pages of the book, crossing out or covering over the back of each facing page of the novel's text. Following the lecture he also pasted in a number of poems including "O Captain! My Captain!", with the reading of which Whitman customarily concluded his lecture. The presence of the other poems would seem to bear no relation to the lecture, but suggests that Whitman may have used the volume also in giving "readings" of his own and selections from other writers.

The next year, 1881, Whitman journeyed to Boston to give his lecture, on the invitation of George Parsons Lathrop, Hawthorne's son-in-law. The place and time were the Hawthorne Room of the St. Botolph's Club on the night of April 15. Sylvester Baxter reported the event in a column and a half in the *Boston Herald* of April 16, two paragraphs from which are as follows:

It was a pleasant sight at the Hawthorne rooms on Friday evening; the fine audience representing the best side of Boston literary activity, and the poet, with venerable hair and beard, but sturdy presence, reading his fine essay with the native eloquence born of sincere feeling—just as if reading to a few personal friends—but with none of the tricks of the elocutionizing trade. He has been welcomed to Boston with open arms. Old and young, old friends and new, have gathered around him. The young men have taken to him as one with themselves; as one of those fresh natures that are ever youthful; the older ones, many of whom might once have been disposed to regard him with disfavor, now have grown to see the real core of the man in its soundness and sweetness, and are equally hearty in their welcome. 'He is a grand old fellow' is everybody's verdict. Walt Whitman has in times past been, perhaps, more ignorantly than wilfully misunderstood, but time brings about its revenges, and his present position goes to prove that, let a man be true to himself, however he defies the world, the world will come at last to respect him for his loyalty. Perhaps, frankness may be said to be the keynote of Walt Whitman's nature.

His visit is so pleasant that he says he will repeat it before long. He has been overwhelmed with attentions. Many of the leading literati were at his lecture, and, among them, Mr. Howells was most cordial in his greeting. On Friday afternoon he called on Mr. Longfellow, and Saturday morning he breakfasted with Mr. James T. Fields, where Mrs. Celia Thaxter was also a guest. Many distinguished people have called upon him at the Revere House, and his old friend, Mr. J. T. Trowbridge, has the promise of a visit from him at his home in Arlington the next time he visits Boston.

For the five years from 1880 to 1885 it is not certain where or when Whitman may have given the lecture, if at all. Autograph changes which he made in the first sentence of the clipping which furnishes the first paragraph in the Reading Book indicate that he may have given it in 1885, and certainly did in 1886, and again in 1887. The first change in the right margin in red ink reads "over twenty." Over this he wrote "April 14 15, 1865, 1865." The next change reads "nearly twenty-one years bygone." Then he crossed out "one" and inserted "two," making it read "nearly twenty-two years bygone." In the left margin he wrote "close on twenty-two."

As for 1886 the facts are verifiable. On February 2 Whitman went to Elkton, Maryland, to deliver the lecture. In his diary he noted "the pleasant evening banquet of the Pythian Club was paid $30" (Fein-

CHESTNUT ✦ STREET ✦ OPERA ✦ HOUSE,

Chestnut St., above 10th, Phila.

The Opera House, through the courtesy of Messrs. ZIMMER-
MAN and NIXON, Proprietors and Managers,
and DION BOUCICAULT, Esq.

The Orchestra tendered by SIMON HASSLER, Esq.

Lecture,

By

Walt Whitman,

On

Abraham Lincoln,

THURSDAY AFTERNOON, APRIL 15, '86.

3 o'clock, P. M.

Simon Hassler, Esq., and Hassler's Chestnut Street Opera House Orchestra in the following
Musical Prelude:

1.	Fantasia,—"The Poet's Dream," - - -	*Suppe*
2.	{ Serenade, - - - - - -	*Schubert*
	{ Cornet Solo, - - - -	Mr. Wm. Ewers.
3.	Spanish Fantasia, - - - -	*Missud*

3.20 o'clock, P. M.,

Mr. Whitman's Lecture on Abraham Lincoln.

Program of Whitman's lecture, Philadelphia, April 15, 1886,

O CAPTAIN! MY CAPTAIN!

O Captain! my Captain! our fearful trip is done,
The ship has weather'd every rack, the prize we sought is won,
The port is near, the bells I hear, the people all exulting,
While follow eyes the steady keel, the vessel grim and daring;
  But O heart! heart! heart!
   O the bleeding drops of red,
    Where on the deck my Captain lies,
     Fallen cold and dead.

O Captain! my Captain! rise up and hear the bells;
Rise up—for you the flag is flung—for you the bugle trills,
For you bouquets and ribbon'd wreaths—for you the shores
   a-crowding,
For you they call, the swaying mass, their eager faces turning;
  ~~Hear~~ Captain! dear father! *Here*
   This arm beneath your head!
    It is some dream that on the deck,
     You've fallen cold and dead.

My Captain does not answer, his lips are pale and still,
My father does not feel my arm, he has no pulse nor will,
The ship is anchor'd safe and sound, its voyage closed and done,
From fearful trip the victor ship comes in with object won;
  Exult O shores, and ring O bells!
   But I with mournful tread,
    Walk the deck my Captain lies,
     Fallen cold and dead.

with misprint corrected by Whitman. *Feinberg Collection.*

berg Collection). Again on March 1 he gave the lecture in Camden at Morgan Hall, for which he noted "received $25." But the big occasion this year was his lecture on April 15 at the Chestnut Street Opera House in Philadelphia, for which he prepared a special program showing full page portraits of Lincoln and Whitman on the outside and the program of the afternoon and the complete text of "O Captain! My Captain!" on the inside. The use of the Opera House was donated and he made $687.00 on the occasion. Here reproduced in facsimile from the Feinberg Collection, the program shows Whitman's correction of a misprint in the second stanza of the poem.

The first paragraph of the reading copy is a much revised clipping from the *Camden Daily Post,* April 16, 1880, which printed the text for his Association Hall lecture. Originally Whitman had pasted in this first paragraph as set in type for the Association Hall lecture, and this remained, apparently, until he gave the lecture at the Chestnut Street Opera House on April 15, 1886. The paragraph as revised for the Association Hall occasion is shown in facsimile together with a ticket of admission. It may be assumed that the newspaper clipping from the *Camden Daily Post* permanently replaced the Association Hall paragraph following the delivery of the lecture at the Chestnut Street Opera House, but the autograph revisions of the clipping suggest that the clipping was revised and used at Elkton, Maryland, on February 2 ("over twenty") and Camden on March 1 ("nearly twenty-one") as well as in 1887 ("close on twenty-two").

On May 18, 1886, Whitman gave the lecture for the fourth time that year, at Haddonfield, New Jersey,

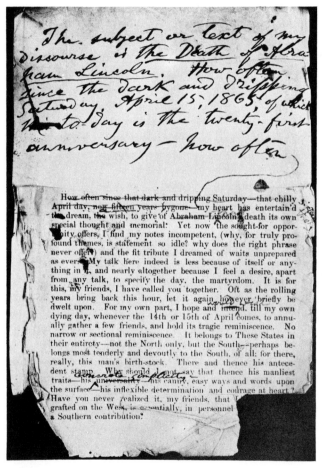

Ticket to Whitman's lecture, Philadelphia, April 15, 1886, and
Whitman's revised introduction to this lecture.
Feinberg Collection.

as his diary entry indicates "without pay—benefit of
a new church building fund at Collingwood."

In 1887 Whitman gave the lecture twice, the first
time on April 5 at the Unity Church in Camden, and
the second at the Madison Square Theatre in New
York on the afternoon of April 14. Arrangements for
this second lecture were principally under the aus-
pices of Major James B. Pond, a leading New York
impresario of "Concerts, Lecturers, And All De-
scriptions of Musical, Lyceum and Literary Entertainments" as indicated by his letterhead, here reproduced from the Feinberg Collection. Pond was assisted by Richard Watson Gilder and other New York
literati in making the most of the occasion.

The lecture was fully reported in the New York
papers, and in 1922 Stuart Merrill published his recollections of the afternoon and the evening reception
that followed. Whitman told John Johnston, who had
helped to organize the lecture, that "the evening reception was the culminating hour of his life." The
audience included: James Russell Lowell, John Burroughs, Charles Eliot Norton, Edmund Stedman and
his family, Samuel L. Clemens, H. C. Bunner, Frank
Stockton, Moncure D. Conway, Joel Benton, John
Hay, Edward Eggleston, Andrew Carnegie, Augus-
tus St. Gaudens, Mrs. Frances Hodgson Burnett, Mrs.
Mary Mapes Dodge, President Gilman of Johns Hop-
kins University, Miss Jeanette Gilder and many others. Whitman's lecture was occasionally interrupted
by applause. At the close, by way of delicate allusion
to Whitman's great theme on Lincoln, Laura Stedman
—the five year old granddaughter of the banker-poet
—walked out upon the stage and presented Walt
Whitman with a basket of lilac blossoms. Whitman

JAMES B. POND.

GENERAL AGENT AND MANAGER.

EVERETT HOUSE, CORNER 4TH AVENUE AND 17TH STREET, NEW YORK.

SEASON OF 1887-88.

Everett House, New York,   Apr. 25th,   1887.

Walt Whitman, Esq.,

Camden, N. J.

Dear Mr. Whitman:-

Your second postal received. Mr. Gilder told me of Mr. Carnaghie's kind subscription. I congratulate you on your remarkable success.

How would you like to go to Boston about Tuesday, May 10th? That would be a good time. If this meets your approval let me know and I will fix the date.

I have had some very nice letters from Holmes, Norton, Grant, and others, expressing the wish that you will visit the "hub".

Yours Sincerely,

J. B. Pond

I am now booking time for Mr. Henry George for next season. Associations desiring him will find it to their advantage to apply early.

Please do not write letters on Postal Cards. They are liable to get overlooked - J. B. P

Impresario James B. Pond suggests that Whitman lecture in Boston. *Feinberg Collection.*

then recited "O Captain!" and the curtain fell amid warm applause. In the evening, at least 250 admirers called upon him in the parlours of the Westminster Hotel. Walt Whitman autographed the printed "At Home" cards, in many instances not correcting the date which was printed "15th" instead of April 14th.

For this lecture Whitman received from Pond $250 from admissions collected, and from Andrew Carnegie a check for $350, forwarded by Richard Watson Gilder, in payment for Carnegie's box. In fact, the lecture was so successful that Pond wrote Whitman on April 25 with the suggestion of a repeat performance in Boston "about Tuesday May 10," but Whitman did not accept.

Although Whitman did not lecture on Lincoln in 1888 or 1889 so far as has been discovered, he sent his last Lincoln poem to the *New York Herald* on February 10, 1888. It was published on February 12.

Abraham Lincoln, Born Feb. 12, 1809.
To-day, from each and all, a breath of prayer—a pulse of thought,
To memory of him—to birth of him.

On Sunday, April 15, Whitman had dinner at Thomas B. Harned's with Horace Traubel. Raising his glass and glancing at the picture of Lincoln, he gave a toast: "Here's to the blessed man . . . . You know this is the day he died: After my dear, dear mother, I guess Lincoln gets almost nearer me than anybody else." (Traubel, *With Walt Whitman in Camden,* 1906, I, 38) Also in 1888 appeared Whitman's contribution to the *North American Review's* "Reminiscences of Abraham Lincoln" edited by Allen Thorndike Rice, which had been originally

Whitman's account of his last lecture, Philadelphia, April 15, 1890. *Feinberg Collection.*

Whitman's introduction to his final lecture, Philadelphia, April 15, 1890. *Feinberg Collection.*

Whitman's comments about himself, April 15, 1890.
Feinberg Collection.

solicited by James Redpath in a letter to Whitman dated July 16, 1885.

Mr. Rice has got the ambition of editing a work that *can* never be superseded. He proposes to get every man of note now living who ever met Lincoln to write down in plain words and as accurately as the human memory will record, just what Lincoln did; just how Lincoln looked; just what impression Lincoln made on him. However, he does *not* want the last clause, (that is to say the impressions) recorded by anybody but only by men whose names will go down to history. Like Gradgrind, 'what he wants is *facts.*' You, of course, are among the favored few whose impressions will be acceptable; so, you see, if you will write down an account of every interview you ever had with Lincoln, *that* will complete what I ask of you in his name on that subject. [Original owned by Charles E. Feinberg]

The letter continues with a second request for ''an account of some phase of the Civil War which you witnessed.'' Whitman delivered both articles. The Lincoln piece was his last writing about the Civil War President with the exception of the autograph additions to his lecture for its final delivery on April 15, 1890, as shown in the facsimile of the Reading Book, and the account of this last lecture which he sent to his friend William Sloane Kennedy for publication in the *Boston Transcript.*

ROY P. BASLER

Library of Congress

ACKNOWLEDGMENT

THE preparation of this little book would have been completely impossible without the cooperation and friendly advice of Charles E. Feinberg, the riches of whose collection of Whitman material are surpassed only by his generosity and his intimate knowledge of Whitman.

Thanks are also due and gladly rendered to the following for permission to reproduce items from their respective Whitman collections: Yale University Library, Van Sinderen Collection; Henry E. Huntington Library, Nicholson Collection; and the Library of Congress, Harned Collection.

Information and assistance were likewise forthcoming from Herbert Cahoon, Curator, Autograph Manuscripts, The Pierpont Morgan Library; Donald C. Gallup, Curator, Collection of American Literature, Yale University Library; Robert W. Hill, Keeper of Manuscripts, The New York Public Library; John H. Lancaster, Librarian, Slocum Library, Ohio Wesleyan University; Benjamin E. Powell, Librarian, Duke University; Herbert C. Schulz, Curator of Manuscripts, and Carey S. Bliss, Assistant Curator of Rare Books, Henry E. Huntington Library and Art Gallery; John Cook Wyllie, Librarian, and Miss Anne Freudenberg, Assistant in Manuscripts, Alderman Library, University of Virginia.

Other librarians and collectors have contributed information as indicated in the check list of extant copies of *Memoranda During the War*.

R. P. B.

Extant Copies of *Memoranda During the War*

OF twenty-two "Remembrance Copies" that have been located, Mr. Charles E. Feinberg owns 6, Yale University Library 3, New York Public Library 3, and one is in the collections of each of the following: Mr. John D. Gordon, Mr. Carl Haverlin, Henry E. Huntington Library, Alderman Library of the University of Virginia, Ohio Wesleyan University Library, Duke University Library, Houghton Library of Harvard University, University of Pennsylvania Library, Northwestern University Library, University of Texas Library.

Of eleven copies without preliminary pages preceding the title page that have been located, Mr. Charles E. Feinberg possesses one (unbound), and each of the following possesses one: Mr. Gay W. Allen, Mr. Carl Haverlin, Pierpont Morgan Library, Alderman Library of the University of Virginia, University of Chicago Library, Library Company of Philadelphia, University of Michigan Library, Newberry Library, Southern Illinois University Library, Syracuse University Library.

MEMORANDA DURING THE WAR

Remembrance Copy.

TO *J. H. Johnston*

From *his friend* *the Author*

1877

PERSONAL--NOTE.

Dear Friend :

I do not hesitate to briefly precede your Remembrance-Copy with some biographical facts of myself, I know you will like to have—also, to bind in, for your eye and thought, the little Portraits that follow*.

I was born May 31, 1819, in my father's farm-house, at West Hills, L. I., New York State. My parents' folks mostly farmers and sailors—on my father's side, of English—on my mother's, (Van Velsor's,) from Hollandic immigration.

We moved to Brooklyn while I was still a little one in frocks—and there in B. I grew up out of the frocks—then, as child and boy, went to the public schools—then to work in a printing office.†

When only sixteen or seventeen years old, and for two years afterward, I went to teaching country schools down in Queens and Suffolk counties, Long Island, and "boarded round." Then, returning to New York, worked as printer and writer, (with an occasional shy at "poetry.")

---

* The picture in shirt-sleeves was daguerreotyped from life, one hot day in August, 1855, by my friend Gabriel Harrison, in Fulton St., Brooklyn—and here drawn on steel by McRae—(was a very faithful and characteristic likeness at the time.) The head that follows was photographed from life, Washington, 1872, by Geo. C. Potter, here drawn on wood by W. J. Linton.

† There was, first and last, a large family of children ; (I was the second.) Besides those mentioned above, were my elder brother Jesse, my dear sister Mary, my brother Andrew, and then my youngest brother Edward, (always badly crippled—as I now am of late years.)

PERSONAL—NOTE.

1848–'9.—**About this time went off on a leisurely journey** and working expedition (my brother Jeff with me,) through all the Middle States, and down the Ohio and Mississippi rivers. Lived a while in New Orleans, and worked there. After a time, plodded back northward, up the Mississippi, the Missouri, &c., and around to, and by way of, the great lakes, Michigan, Huron and Erie, to Niagara falls and lower Canada—finally returning through Central New York, and down the Hudson.

1851–'54.—**Occupied in house-building in Brooklyn.** (For a little of the first part of that time in printing a daily and weekly paper.)

1855.—**Lost my dear father, this year, by death....** Commenced putting *Leaves of Grass* to press, for good—after many MS. doings and undoings—(I had great trouble in leaving out the stock "poetical" touches—but succeeded at last.)

1862.—**In December of this year went down to the field of** War in Virginia. My brother George, reported badly wounded, in the Fredericksburgh fight. (For 1863 and '64, see my *Memoranda* following.)

1865 to '71.—**Had a place as clerk (till '74) in the Attorney** General's Office, Washington.

(**New York and Brooklyn seem more like *home*, as I was** born near, and brought up in them, and lived, man and boy, for 30 years. But I lived some years in Washington, and have visited most of the Western and Eastern cities.)

1872.—**Took a two months' trip through the New England** States, up the Connecticut valley, Vermont, the Adirondack region—and to Burlington, to see my dear sister Hannah once more. Returning, had a pleasant day-trip down Lake Champlain—and, the next day, down the Hudson.

1873.—**This year lost, by death, my dear, dear mother—** and, just before, my sister Martha—(the two best and sweetest women I have ever seen or known, or ever expect to see.)

Same year, paralyzed. Quit work at Washington, and moved to Camden, New Jersey—where I now (April, 1876) write these lines.

W. W.

MEMORANDA

During the War.

BY WALT WHITMAN.

Author's Publication.

CAMDEN, NEW JERSEY

1875—'76.

NEW REPUBLIC PRINT,
Federal St., Camden

MEMORANDA, &c.

During the Union War I commenced at the close of 1862,
and continued steadily through '63, '64 and '65, to visit the
sick and wounded of the Army, both on the field and in the
Hospitals in and around Washington city. From the first I
kept little note-books for impromptu jottings in pencil to re-
fresh my memory of names and circumstances, and what was
specially wanted, &c. In these I brief'd cases, persons,
sights, occurrences in camp, by the bedside, and not seldom
by the corpses of the dead. Of the present Volume most of
its pages are *verbatim* renderings from such pencillings on
the spot. Some were scratch'd down from narratives I heard
and itemized while watching, or waiting, or tending somebody amid those scenes. I have perhaps forty such little
note-books left, forming a special history of those years, for
myself alone, full of associations never to be possibly said
or sung. I wish I could convey to the reader the associations that attach to these soil'd and creas'd little livraisons,
each composed of a sheet or two of paper, folded small to
carry in the pocket, and fasten'd with a pin. I leave them
just as I threw them by during the War, blotch'd here and
there with more than one blood-stain, hurriedly written,
sometimes at the clinique, not seldom amid the excitement
of uncertainty, or defeat, or of action, or getting ready for it,
or a march. Even these days, at the lapse of many years, I
can never turn their tiny leaves, or even take one in my
hand, without the actual army sights and hot emotions of the
time rushing like a river in full tide through me. Each line,
each scrawl, each memorandum, has its history. Some pang
of anguish—some tragedy, profounder than ever poet wrote.
Out of them arise active and breathing forms. They sum-
mon up, even in this silent and vacant room as I write, not
only the sinewy regiments and brigades, marching or in
camp, but the countless phantoms of those who fell and were
hastily buried by wholesale in the battle-pits, or whose dust
and bones have been since removed to the National Cemeteries of the land, especially through Virginia and Tennessee. (Not Northern soldiers only—many indeed the Caro-
linian, Georgian, Alabamian, Louisianian, Virginian—many
a Southern face and form, pale, emaciated, with that strange
tie of confidence and love between us, welded by sickness,
pain of wounds, and little daily, nightly offices of nursing and
friendly words and visits, comes up amid the rest, and does

not mar, but rounds and gives a finish to the meditation.)
Vivid as life, they recall and identify the long Hospital
Wards, with their myriad-varied scenes of day or night—the
graphic incidents of field or camp—the night before the battle, with many solemn yet cool preparations—the changeful
exaltations and depressions of those four years, North and
South—the convulsive memories, (let but a word, a broken
sentence, serve to recall them)—the clues already quite van-
ish'd, like some old dream, and yet the list significant enough
to soldiers—the scrawl'd, worn slips of paper that came up
by bushels from the Southern prisons, Salisbury or Anderson-
ville, by the hands of exchanged prisoners—the clank of
crutches on the pavements or floors of Washington, or up
and down the stairs of the Paymasters' offices—the Grand
Review of homebound veterans at the close of the War,
cheerily marching day after day by the President's house,
one brigade succeeding another until it seem'd as if they
would never end—the strange squads of Southern deserters, (*escapees*, I call'd them;)—that little *genre* group, un-
reck'd amid the mighty whirl, I remember passing in a hospital corner, of a dying Irish boy, a Catholic priest, and an
improvised altar—Four years compressing centuries of native
passion, first-class pictures, tempests of life and death—an
inexhaustible mine for the Histories, Drama, Romance and
even Philosophy of centuries to come—indeed the Verteber
of Poetry and Art, (of personal character too,) for all future
America, (far more grand, in my opinion, to the hands
capable of it, than Homer's siege of Troy, or the French
wars to Shakspere;)—and looking over all, in my remembrance, the tall form of President Lincoln, with his face of
deep-cut lines, with the large, kind, canny eyes, the complexion of dark brown, and the tinge of wierd melancholy
saturating all.

More and more, in my recollections of that period, and
through its varied, multitudinous oceans and murky whirls,
appear the central resolution and sternness of the bulk of
the average American People, animated in Soul by a definite purpose, though sweeping and fluid as some great
storm—the Common People, emblemised in thousands of
specimens of first-class Heroism, steadily accumulating, (no
regiment, no company, hardly a file of men, North or South,
the last three years, without such first-class specimens.)

I know not how it may have been, or may be, to others—
to me the main interest of the War, I found, (and still, on
recollection, find,) in those specimens, and in the ambulance,
the Hospital, and even the dead on the field. To me, the
points illustrating the latent Personal Character and eligi-
bilities of These States, in the two or three millions of American young and middle-aged men, North and South, embodied
in the armies—and especially the one-third or one-fourth of

their number, stricken by wounds or disease at some time in the course of the contest—were of more significance even than the Political interests involved. (As so much of a Race depends on what it thinks of death, and how it stands personal anguish and sickness. As, in the glints of emotions under emergencies, and the indirect traits and asides in Plutarch, &c., we get far profounder clues to the antique world than all its more formal history.)

Future years will never know the seething hell and the black infernal background of countless minor scenes and interiors, (not the few great battles) of the Secession War ; and it is best they should not. In the mushy influences of current times the fervid atmosphere and typical events of those years are in danger of being totally forgotten. I have at night watch'd by the side of a sick man in the hospital, one who could not live many hours. I have seen his eyes flash and burn as he recurr'd to the cruelties on his surrender'd brother, and mutilations of the corpse afterward. [See, in the following pages, the incident at Upperville—the seventeen, kill'd as in the description, were left there on the ground. After they dropt dead, no one touch'd them—all were made sure of, however. The carcasses were left for the citizens to bury or not, as they chose.]

Such was the War. It was not a quadrille in a ball-room. Its interior history will not only never be written, its practicality, minutia of deeds and passions, will never be even suggested. The actual Soldier of 1862-'65, North and South, with all his ways, his incredible dauntlessness, habits, practices, tastes, language, his appetite, rankness, his superb strength and animality, lawless gait, and a hundred unnamed lights and shades of camp—I say, will never be written—perhaps must not and should not be.

The present Memoranda may furnish a few stray glimpses into that life, and into those lurid interiors of the period, never to be fully convey'd to the future. For that purpose, and for what goes along with it, the Hospital part of the drama from '61 to '65, deserves indeed to be recorded—(I but suggest it.) Of that many-threaded drama, with its sudden and strange surprises, its confounding of prophecies, its moments of despair, the dread of foreign interference, the interminable campaigns, the bloody battles, the mighty and cumbrous and green armies, the drafts and bounties—the immense money expenditure, like a heavy pouring constant rain—with, over the whole land, the last three years of the struggle, an unending, universal mourning-wail of women, parents, orphans—the marrow of the tragedy concentrated in those Hospitals—(it seem'd sometimes as if the whole interest of the land, North and South, was one vast central Hospital, and all the rest of the affair but flanges)—those forming the Untold and Unwritten History of the War—infinitely greater (like Life's) than the few scraps and distortions that are ever told or written. Think how much, and of importance, will be—how much, civic and military, has already been—buried in the grave, in eternal darkness !....... But to my Memoranda.

FALMOUTH, VA., *opposite Fredericksburgh, December* 21, 1862.—Began my visits among the Camp Hospitals in the Army of the Potomac. Spent a good part of the day in a large brick mansion, on the banks of the Rappahannock, used as a Hospital since the battle—Seems to have receiv'd only the worst cases. Out doors, at the foot of a tree, within ten yards of the front of the house, I notice a heap of amputated feet, legs, arms, hands, &c., a full load for a one-horse cart. Several dead bodies lie near, each cover'd with its brown woollen blanket. In the door-yard, towards the river, are fresh graves, mostly of officers, their names on pieces of barrel-staves or broken board, stuck in the dirt. (Most of these bodies were subsequently taken up and transported North to their friends.)..........The large mansion is quite crowded, upstairs and down, everything impromptu, no system, all bad enough, but I have no doubt the best that can be done ; all the wounds pretty bad, some frightful, the men in their old clothes, unclean and bloody. Some of the wounded are rebel soldiers and officers, prisoners. One, a Mississippian—a captain—hit badly in leg, I talk'd with some time ; he ask'd me for papers, which I gave him. (I saw him three months afterward in Washington, with his leg amputated, doing well.)..........I went through the rooms, downstairs and up. Some of the men were dying. I had nothing to give at that visit, but wrote a few letters to folks home, mothers, &c. Also talk'd to three or four, who seem'd most susceptible to it, and needing it.

(Everything is quiet now, here about Falmouth and the Rappahannock, but there was noise enough a week or so ago. Probably the earth never shook by artificial means, nor the air reverberated, more than on that winter daybreak of eight or nine days since, when Gen. Burnside order'd all the batteries of the army to combine for the bombardment of Fredericksburgh. It was in its way the most magnificent and terrible spectacle, with all the adjunct of sound, throughout the War. The perfect hush of the just-ending night was suddenly broken by the first gun, and in an instant all the thunderers, big and little, were in full chorus, which they kept up without intermission for several hours.)

December 23 *to* 31.—The results of the late battles are exhibited everywhere about here in thousands of cases, (hundreds die every day,) in the Camp, Brigade, and Division Hospitals. These are merely tents, and sometimes very poor ones, the wounded lying on the ground, lucky if their blankets are spread on layers of pine or hemlock twigs or small leaves. No cots ; seldom even a mattress. It is pretty cold. The ground is frozen hard, and there is occasional snow. I go around from one case to another. I do not see that I do much good, but I cannot leave them. Once in a while some youngster holds on to me convulsively, and I do what I can for him ; at any rate, stop with him and sit near him for hours, if he wishes it.

Besides the hospitals, I also go occasionally on long tours through the camps, talking with the men, &c. Sometimes at night among the groups around the fires, in their shebang enclosures of bushes. These are curious shows, full of characters and groups. I soon get acquainted anywhere in camp, with officers or men, and am always well used. Sometimes I go down on picket with the regiments I know best........As to rations, the army here at present seems to be tolerably well supplied, and the men have enough, such as it is, mainly salt pork and hard tack. Most of the regiments lodge in the flimsy little shelter-tents. A few have built themselves huts of logs and mud, with fireplaces.

WASHINGTON, *January*, '63.—Left camp at Falmouth, with some wounded, a few days since, and came here by Aquia Creek railroad, and so on Government steamer up the Potomac. Many wounded were with us on the cars and boat. The cars were just common platform ones. The railroad journey of ten or twelve miles was made mostly before sunrise. The soldiers guarding the road came out from their tents or shebangs of bushes with rumpled hair and half-awake look. Those on duty were walking their posts, some on banks over us, others down far below the level of the track. I saw large cavalry camps off the road. At Aquia Creek landing were numbers of wounded going North. While I waited some three hours, I went around among them. Several wanted word sent home to parents, brothers, wives, &c., which I did for them, (by mail the next day from Washington.) On the boat I had my hands full. One poor fellow died going up.

I am now remaining in and around Washington, daily visiting the hospitals. Am much in Patent Office, Eighth street, H street, Armory Square and others. Am now able to do a little good, having money, (as almoner of others home,) and getting experience........To-day, Sunday afternoon and till nine in the evening, visited Campbell Hospital ; attended specially to one case in Ward 1 ; very sick with pleurisy and typhoid fever ; young man, farmer's son, D. F. Russell, Company E, Sixtieth New York ; downhearted and feeble ; a long time before he would take any interest ; wrote a letter home to his mother, in Malone, Franklin County, N. Y., at his request ; gave him some fruit and one or two other gifts ; envelop'd and directed his letter, &c Then went thoroughly through Ward 6 ; observ'd every

case in the Ward, without, I think, missing one ; gave perhaps from twenty to thirty persons, each one some little
gift, such as oranges, apples, sweet crackers, figs, &c.

Thursday, *Jan.* 21.—Devoted the main part of the day to
Armory Square Hospital ; went pretty thoroughly through
Wards F, G, H, and I ; some fifty cases in each Ward. In
Ward F supplied the men throughout with writing paper
and stamp'd envelope each ; distributed in small portions,
to proper subjects, a large jar of first-rate preserv'd berries,
which had been donated to me by a lady—her own cooking.
Found several cases I thought good subjects for small sums
of money, which I furnish'd. (The wounded men often
come up broke, and it helps their spirits to have even the
small sum I give them.) My paper and envelopes all gone,
but distributed a good lot of amusing reading matter ; also,
as I thought judicious, tobacco, oranges, apples, &c. Interesting cases in Ward I ; Charles Miller, bed No. 19, Company D, Fifty-third Pennsylvania, is only sixteen years of
age, very bright, courageous boy, left leg amputated below
the knee ; next bed to him, another young lad very sick ;
gave each appropriate gifts. In the bed above, also, amputation of the left leg ; gave him a little jar of raspberries ;
bed No. 1, this Ward, gave a small sum ; also to a soldier on
crutches, sitting on his bed near.......(I am more and more
surprised at the very great proportion of youngsters from
fifteen to twenty-one in the army. I afterwards found a still
greater proportion among the Southerners.)

Evening, same day, went to see D. F. R., before alluded
to ; found him remarkably changed for the better ; up and
dress'd—quite a triumph ; he afterwards got well, and went
back to his regiment.........Distributed in the Wards a
quantity of note-paper, and forty or fifty stamp'd envelopes,
of which I had recruited my stock, and the men were much
in need.

Fifty Hours Left Wounded on the Field.—Here is a case
of a soldier I found among the crowded cots in the Patent
Office. He likes to have some one to talk to, and we will
listen to him. He got badly hit in his leg and side at Fredericksburgh that eventful Saturday, 13th of December. He
lay the succeeding two days and nights helpless on the field,
between the city and those grim terraces of batteries ; his
company and regiment had been compell'd to leave him to
his fate. To make matters worse, it happen'd he lay with
his head slightly down hill, and could not help himself. At
the end of some fifty hours he was brought off, with other
wounded, under a flag of truce.........I ask him how the
rebels treated him as he lay during those two days and nights
within reach of them—whether they came to him—whether
they abused him ? He answers that several of the rebels,
soldiers and others, came to him, at one time and another.

A couple of them, who were together, spoke roughly and sarcastically, but nothing worse. One middle-aged man, however, who seem'd to be moving around the field, among the dead and wounded, for benevolent purposes, came to him in a way he will never forget; treated our soldier kindly, bound up his wounds, cheer'd him, gave him a couple of biscuits, and a drink of whiskey and water ; ask'd him if he could eat some beef. This good Secesh, however, did not change our soldier's position, for it might have caused the blood to burst from the wounds, clotted and stagnated. Our soldier is from Pennsylvania; has had a pretty severe time ; the wounds proved to be bad ones. But he retains a good heart, and is at present on the gain.........(It is not uncommon for the men to remain on the field this way, one, two, or even four or five days.)

Letter Writing.—When eligible, I encourage the men to write, and myself, when call'd upon, write all sorts of letters for them, (including love letters, very tender ones.) Almost as I reel off this memoranda, I write for a new patient to his wife. M. de F., of the Seventeenth Connecticut, Company H, has just come up (February 17) from Windmill Point, and is received in Ward H, Armory Square. He is an intelligent looking man, has a foreign accent, black-eyed and hair'd, a Hebraic appearance. Wants a telegraphic message sent to his wife, New Canaan, Ct. I agree to send the message—but to make things sure, I also sit down and write the wife a letter, and despatch it to the post-office immediately, as he fears she will come on, and he does not wish her to, as he will surely get well.

Saturday, Jan. 30.—Afternoon, visited Campbell Hospital. Scene of cleaning up the Ward, and giving the men all clean clothes—through the Ward (6) the patients dressing or being dress'd—the naked upper half of the bodies—the good-humor and fun—the shirts, drawers, sheets of beds, &c., and the general fixing up for Sunday. Gave J. L. 50 cts.

Wednesday, Feb. 4th.—Visited Armory Square Hospital, went pretty thoroughly through Wards E and D. Supplied paper and envelopes to all who wish'd—as usual, found plenty of the men who needed those articles. Wrote letters. Saw and talk'd with two or three members of the Brooklyn Fourteenth.........A poor fellow in Ward D, with a fearful wound in a fearful condition, was having some loose splinters of bone taken from the neighborhood of the wound. The operation was long, and one of great pain—yet, after it was well commenced, the soldier bore it in silence. He sat up, propp'd—was much wasted—had lain a long time quiet in one position, (not for days only, but weeks,)—a bloodless, brown-skinn'd face, with eyes full of determination—belong'd to a New York regiment. There was an unusual cluster of surgeons, medical cadets, nurses, &c., around his bed—I

2

thought the whole thing was done with tenderness, and done well.

In one case, the wife sat by the side of her husband, his sickness, typhoid fever, pretty bad. In another, by the side of her son—a mother—she told me she had seven children, and this was the youngest. (A fine, kind, healthy, gentle mother, good-looking, not very old, with a cap on her head, and dress'd like home—what a charm it gave to the whole Ward.) I liked the woman nurse in Ward E—I noticed how she sat a long time by a poor fellow who just had, that morning, in addition to his other sickness, bad hemmorhage —she gently assisted him, reliev'd him of the blood, holding a cloth to his mouth, as he cough'd it up—he was so weak he could only just turn his head over on the pillow.

One young New York man, with a bright, handsome face, had been lying several months from a most disagreeable wound, receiv'd at Bull Run. A bullet had shot him right through the bladder, hitting him front, low in the belly, and coming out back. He had suffer'd much—the water came out of the wound. by slow but steady quantities, for many weeks—so that he lay almost constantly in a sort of puddle—and there were other disagreeable circumstances. He was of good heart, however. At present comparatively comfortable ; had a bad throat, was delighted with a stick of horehound candy I gave him, with one or two other trifles.

Feb. 23.—I must not let the great Hospital at the Patent Office pass away without some mention. A few weeks ago the vast area of the second story of that noblest of Washington buildings, was crowded close with rows of sick, badly wounded and dying soldiers. They were placed in three very large apartments. I went there many times. It was a strange, solemn and, with all its features of suffering and death, a sort of fascinating sight. I go sometimes at night to soothe and relieve particular cases. Two of the immense apartments are fill'd with high and ponderous glass cases, crowded with models in miniature of every kind of utensil, machine or invention, it ever enter'd into the mind of man to conceive ; and with curiosities and foreign presents. Between these cases are lateral openings, perhaps eight feet wide, and quite deep, and in these were placed the sick ; besides a great long double row of them up and down through the middle of the hall. Many of them were very bad cases, wounds and amputations. Then there was a gallery running above the hall, in which there were beds also. It was, indeed, a curious scene at night, when lit up. The glass cases, the beds, the forms lying there, the gallery above, and the marble pavement under foot—the suffering, and the fortitude to bear it in various degrees—occasionally, from some, the groan that could not be repress'd—sometimes a poor fellow dying, with emaciated face and glassy eye, the nurse by his side, the doctor also there, but no friend, no relative—such were the sights but lately in the Patent Office. The wounded have since been removed from there, and it is now vacant again.

The White House, by Moonlight—Feb. 24.—A spell of fine soft weather. I wander about a good deal, especially at night, under the moon. To-night took a long look at the President's House—and here is my splurge about it. The white portico—the brilliant gas-light shining—the palace-like portico—the tall, round columns, spotless as snow—the walls also—the tender and soft moonlight, flooding the pale marble, and making peculiar faint languishing shades, not shadows—everywhere too a soft transparent haze, a thin blue moon-lace, hanging in the night in the air—the brilliant and extra plentiful clusters of gas, on and around the facade, columns, portico, &c.—everything so white, so marbly pure and dazzling, yet soft—the White House of future poems, and of dreams and dramas, there in the soft and copious moon—the pure and gorgeous front, in the trees, under the night-lights, under the lustrous flooding moon, full of reality, full of illusion—The forms of the trees, leafless, silent, in trunk and myriad-angles of branches, under the stars and sky—the White House of the land, the White House of the night, and of beauty and silence—sentries at the gates, and by the portico, silent, pacing there in blue overcoats—stopping you not at all, but eyeing you with sharp eyes, whichever way you move.

An Army Hospital Ward.—Let me specialize a visit I made to the collection of barrack-like one-story edifices, call'd Campbell Hospital, out on the flats, at the end of the then horse-railway route, on Seventh street. There is a long building appropriated to each Ward. Let us go into Ward 6. It contains to-day, I should judge, eighty or a hundred patients, half sick, half wounded. The edifice is nothing but boards, well whitewash'd inside, and the usual slender-framed iron bedsteads, narrow and plain. You walk down the central passage, with a row on either side, their feet toward you, and their heads to the wall. There are fires in large stoves, and the prevailing white of the walls is reliev'd by some ornaments, stars, circles, &c., made of evergreens. The view of the whole edifice and occupants can be taken at once, for there is no partition. You may hear groans, or other sounds of unendurable suffering, from two or three of the iron cots, but in the main there is quiet—almost a painful absence of demonstration; but the pallid face, the dull'd eye, and the moisture on the lip, are demonstration enough. Most of these sick or hurt are evidently young fellows from the country, farmers' sons, and such like. Look at the fine large frames, the bright and broad countenances, and the many yet lingering proofs of strong constitution and physique.

Look at the patient and mute manner of our American wounded, as they lie in such a sad collection ; representatives from all New England, and from New York and New Jersey and Pennsylvania—indeed, from all the States and all the cities—largely from the West. Most of them are entirely without friends or acquaintances here—no familiar face, and hardly a word of judicious sympathy or cheer, through their sometimes long and tedious sickness, or the pangs of aggravated wounds.

A Connecticut Case.—This young man in bed 25 is H. D. B., of the Twenty-seventh Connecticut, Company B. His folks live at Northford, near New Haven. Though not more than twenty-one, or thereabouts, he has knock'd much around the world, on sea and land, and has seen some fighting on both. When I first saw him he was very sick, with no appetite. He declined offers of money—said he did not need anything. As I was quite anxious to do something, he confess'd that he had a hankering for a good home-made rice pudding— thought he could relish it better than anything. At this time his stomach was very weak. (The doctor, whom I consulted, said nourishment would do him more good than anything ; but things in the hospital, though better than usual, revolted him.) I soon procured B. his rice-pudding. A Washington lady, (Mrs. O'C.), hearing his wish, made the pudding herself, and I took it up to him the next day. He subsequently told me he lived upon it for three or four days.......This B. is a good sample of the American Eastern young man—the typical Yankee. I took a fancy to him, and gave him a nice pipe, for a keepsake. He receiv'd afterwards a box of things from home, and nothing would do but I must take dinner with him, which I did, and a very good one it was.

Two Brooklyn Boys.—Here in this same Ward are two young men from Brooklyn, members of the Fifty-first New York. I had known both the two as young lads at home, so they seem near to me. One of them, J. L., lies there with an amputated arm, the stump healing pretty well. (I saw him lying on the ground at Fredericksburgh last December, all bloody, just after the arm was taken off. He was very phlegmatic about it, munching away at a cracker in the remaining hand—made no fuss.) He will recover, and thinks and talks yet of meeting the Johnny Rebs.

A Secesh Brave.—The brave, grand soldiers are not comprised in those of one side, any more than the other. Here is a sample of an unknown Scutherner, a lad of seventeen. At the War Department, a few days ago, I witness'd a presentation of captured flags to the Secretary. Among others a soldier named Gant, of the One Hundred and Fourth Ohio Volunteers, presented a rebel battle-flag, which one of the officers stated to me was borne to the mouth of our cannon and planted there by a boy but seventeen years of age, who

actually endeavor'd to stop the muzzle of the gun with fence-
rails. He was kill'd in the effort, and the flag-staff was sev-
er'd by a shot from one of our men. (Perhaps, in that
Southern boy of seventeen, untold in history, unsung in
poems, altogether unnamed, fell as strong a spirit, and as
sweet, as any in all time.)

The Wounded from Chancellorsville, May, '63.—As I write
this, the wounded have begun to arrive from Hooker's command from bloody Chancellorsville. I was down among the
first arrivals. The men in charge of them told me the bad
cases were yet to come. If that is so I pity them, for
these are bad enough. You ought to see the scene of the
wounded arriving at the landing here foot of Sixth street, at
night. Two boat loads came about half-past seven last
night. A little after eight it rain'd a long and violent
shower. The poor, pale, helpless soldiers had been debark'd,
and lay around on the wharf and neighborhood anywhere.
The rain was, probably, grateful to them ; at any rate they
were exposed to it. The few torches light up the spectacle.
All around—on the wharf, on the ground, out on side
places—the men are lying on blankets, old quilts, &c., with
bloody rags bound round heads, arms, and legs. The attendants are few, and at night few outsiders also—only a few
hard-work'd transportation men and drivers. (The wounded
are getting to be common, and people grow callous.) The
men, whatever their condition, lie there, and patiently wait
till their turn comes to be taken up. Near by, the ambulances are now arriving in clusters, and one after another is
call'd to back up and take its load. Extreme cases are sent
off on stretchers. The men generally make little or no ado,
whatever their sufferings. A few groans that cannot be sup-
press'd, and occasionally a scream of pain as they lift a man
into the ambulance........To day, as I write, hundreds more
are expected, and to-morrow and the next day more, and so
on for many days. Quite often they arrive at the rate of
1000 a day.

May 12—A Night Battle, over a week since.—We already
talk of Histories of the War, (presently to accumulate)—yes
—technical histories of some things, statistics, official reports, and so on—but shall we ever get histories of the *real*
things ?.......There was part of the late battle at Chancellorsville, (second Fredericksburgh,) a little over a week ago,
Saturday, Saturday night and Sunday, under Gen. Joe
Hooker, I would like to give just a glimpse of—(a moment's
look in a terrible storm at sea—of which a few suggestions
are enough, and full details impossible.) The fighting had
been very hot during the day, and after an intermission the
latter part, was resumed at night, and kept up with furious
energy till 3 o'clock in the morning. That afternoon (Saturday) an attack sudden and strong by Stonewall Jackson had

gain'd a great advantage to the Southern army, and broken our lines, entering us like a wedge, and leaving things in that position at dark. But Hooker at 11 at night made a desperate push, drove the Secesh forces back, restored his original lines, and resumed his plans. This night scrimmage was very exciting, and afforded countless strange and fearful pictures. The fighting had been general both at Chancellorsville and northeast at Fredericksburgh. (We hear of some poor fighting, episodes, skedaddling on our part. I think not of it. I think of the fierce bravery, the general rule.) One Corps, the 6th, Sedgewick's, fights four dashing and bloody battles in 36 hours, retreating in great jeopardy, losing largely and maintaining itself, fighting with the sternest desperation under all circumstances, getting over the Rappahannock only by the skin of its teeth, yet getting over. It lost many, many brave men, yet it took vengeance, ample vengeance.

But it was the tug of Saturday evening, and through the night and Sunday morning, I wanted to make a special note of. It was largely in the woods, and quite a general engagement. The night was very pleasant, at times the moon shining out full and clear, all Nature so calm in itself, the early summer grass so rich, and foliage of the trees—yet there the battle raging, and many good fellows lying helpless, with new accessions to them, and every minute amid the rattle of muskets and crash of cannon, (for there was an artillery contest too,) the red life-blood oozing out from heads or trunks or limbs upon that green and dew-cool grass. The woods take fire, and many of the wounded, unable to move, (especially some of the divisions in the Sixth Corps,) are consumed—quite large spaces are swept over, burning the dead also—some of the men have their hair and beards singed—some, splatches of burns on their faces and hands—others holes burnt in their clothing........The flashes of fire from the cannon, the quick flaring flames and smoke, and the immense roar—the musketry so general, the light nearly bright enough for each side to see one another—the crashing, tramping of men—the yelling—close quarters—we hear the Secesh yells—our men cheer loudly back, especially if Hooker is in sight—hand to hand conflicts, each side stands up to it, brave, determin'd as demons, they often charge upon us—a thousand deeds are done worth to write newer greater poems on—and still the woods on fire—still many are not only scorch'd—too many, unable to move, are burn'd to death.........Then the camp of the wounded—O heavens, what scene is this?—is this indeed *humanity*—these butchers' shambles? There are several of them. There they lie, in the largest, in an open space in the woods, from 500 to 600 poor fellows—the groans and screams—the odor of blood, mixed with the fresh scent of the night, the

grass, the trees—that Slaughter-house !—O well is it their
mothers, their sisters cannot see them—cannot conceive, and
never conceiv'd, these things.........One man is shot by a
shell, both in the arm and leg—both are amputated—there
lie the rejected members. Some have their legs blown off—
some bullets through the breast—some indescribably hor-
rid wounds in the face or head, all mutilated, sickening,
torn, gouged out—some in the abdomen—some mere boys—
here is one his face colorless as chalk, lying perfectly still,
a bullet has perforated the abdomen—life is ebbing fast,
there is no help for him. In the camp of the wounded are
many rebels, badly hurt—they take their regular turns with
the rest, just the same as any—the surgeons use them just
the same.........Such is the camp of the wounded—such a
fragment, a reflection afar off of the bloody scene—while
over all the clear, large moon comes out at times softly,
quietly shining.

Such, amid the woods, that scene of flitting souls—amid
the crack and crash and yelling sounds—the impalpable perfume of the woods—and yet the pungent, stifling smoke—
shed with the radiance of the moon, the round, maternal
queen, looking from heaven at intervals so placid—the sky
so heavenly—the clear-obscure up there, those buoyant upper oceans—a few large placid stars beyond, coming out
and then disappearing—the melancholy, draperied night
above, around.......And there, upon the roads, the fields, and
in those woods, that contest, never one more desperate in
any age or land—both parties now in force—masses—no
fancy battle, no semi-play, but fierce and savage demons
fighting there—courage and scorn of death the rule, exceptions almost none.

What history, again I say, can ever give—for who can
know, the mad, determin'd tussle of the armies, in all their
separate large and little squads—as this—each steep'd from
crown to toe in desperate, mortal purports ? Who know the
conflict hand-to-hand—the many conflicts in the dark, those
shadowy-tangled, flashing-moonbeam'd woods—the writhing
groups and squads—hear through the woods the cries, the
din, the cracking guns and pistols—the distant cannon—the
cheers and calls, and threats and awful music of the oaths—
the indiscribable mix—the officers' orders, persuasions, er-
couragements—the devils fully rous'd in human hearts—the
strong word, *Charge, men, charge*—the flash of the naked
sword, and many a flame and smoke—And still the broken,
clear and clouded heaven—and still again the moonlight
pouring silvery soft its radiant patches over all ?.........Who
paint the scene, the sudden partial panic of the afternoon,
at dusk ? Who paint the irrepressible advance of the Second Division of the Third Corps, under Hooker himself,
suddenly order'd up—those rapid-filing phantoms through

the woods? Who show what moves there in the shadows, fluid and firm—to save, (and it did save,) the Army's name, perhaps the Nation? And there the veterans hold the field. (Brave Berry falls not yet—but Death has mark'd him—soon he falls.)

Of scenes like these, I say, who writes—who e'er can write, the story? Of many a score—aye, thousands, North and South, of unwrit heroes, unknown heroisms, incredible, impromptu, first-class desperations—who tells? No history, ever—No poem sings, nor music sounds, those bravest men of all—those deeds. No formal General's report, nor print, nor book in the library, nor column in the paper, embalms the bravest, North or South, East or West. Unnamed, unknown, remain, and still remain, the bravest soldiers. Our manliest—our boys—our hardy darlings. Indeed no picture gives them. Likely their very names are lost. Likely, the typic one of them, (standing, no doubt, for hundreds, thousands,) crawls aside to some bush-clump, or ferny tuft, on receiving his death-shot—there, sheltering a little while, soaking roots, grass and soil with red blood—the battle advances, retreats, flits from the scene, sweeps by—and there, haply with pain and suffering, (yet less, far less, than is supposed,) the last lethargy winds like a serpent round him—the eyes glaze in death—none recks—Perhaps the burial-squads, in truce, a week afterwards, search not the secluded spot—And there, at last, the Bravest Soldier crumbles in the soil of mother earth, unburied and unknown.

June 18.—In one of the Hospitals I find Thomas Haley, Co. M, Fourth New York Cavalry—a regular Irish boy, a fine specimen of youthful physical manliness—shot through the lungs—inevitably dying—came over to this country from Ireland to enlist—has not a single friend or acquaintance here—is sleeping soundly at this moment, (but it is the sleep of death)—has a bullet-hole straight through the lung.......I saw Tom when first brought here, three days since, and didn't supppose he could live twelve hours—(yet he looks well enough in the face to a casual observer.) He lies there with his frame exposed above the waist, all naked, for coolness, a fine built man, the tan not yet bleach'd from his cheeks and neck. It is useless to talk to him, as with his sad hurt, and the stimulants they give him, and the utter strangeness of every object, face, furniture, &c., the poor fellow, even when awake, is like a frighten'd, shy animal. Much of the time he sleeps. or half sleeps. (Sometimes I thought he knew more than he show'd.) I often come and sit by him in perfect silence; he will breathe for ten minutes as softly and evenly as a young babe asleep. Poor youth, so handsome, athletic, with profuse beautiful shining hair. One time as I sat looking at him while he lay asleep, he suddenly, without the least start, awaken'd, open'd his eyes, gave me a long, long steady look, turning his face very slightly to gaze easier—one long, clear silent look—a slight sigh—then turn'd back and went into his doze again.   Little he knew, poor death-stricken boy, the heart of the stranger that hover'd near.

W. H. E., Co. F., Second N. J.—His disease is pneumonia. He lay sick at the wretched hospital below Aquia Creek, for seven or eight days before brought here.   He was detail'd from his regiment to go there and help as nurse ; but was soon taken down himself.   Is an elderly, sallow-faced, rather gaunt, gray-hair'd man ; a widower, with children. He express'd a great desire for good, strong, green tea.   An excellent lady, Mrs. W., of Washington, soon sent him a package ; also a small sum of money.   The doctor said give him the tea at pleasure ; it lay on the table by his side, and he used it every day.   He slept a great deal ; could not talk much, as he grew deaf.   Occupied bed 15, Ward I, Armory. (The same lady above, Mrs. W., sent the men a large package of tobacco.)

J. G. lies in bed 52, Ward I ; is of Co. B, Seventh Pennsylvania.   I gave him a small sum of money, some tobacco and envelopes.   To a man adjoining, also gave 25 cents ; he flush'd in the face, when I offer'd it—refused at first, but as I found he had not a cent, and was very fond of having the daily papers, to read, I prest it on him.   He was evidently very grateful, but said little.

J. T. L., of Co. F., Ninth New Hampshire, lies in bed 37, Ward I.   Is very fond of tobacco.   I furnish him some ; also with a little money.   Has gangrene of the feet, a pretty bad case ; will surely have to lose three toes.   Is a regular specimen of an old-fashion'd, rude, hearty, New England country man, impressing me with his likeness to that celebrated singed cat, who was better than she look'd.

Bed 3, Ward E, Armory, has a great hankering for pickles, something pungent.   After consulting the doctor.   I gave him a small bottle of horse-radish ; also some apples ; also a book.........Some of the nurses are excellent.   The woman nurse in this Ward I like very much.   (Mrs. Wright—a year afterwards I found her in Mansion House Hospital, Alexandri—she is a perfect nurse.)

In one bed a young man, Marcus Small, Co. K, Seventh Maine—sick with dysentery and typhoid fever—pretty critical, too—I talk with him often—he thinks he will die—looks like it indeed.   I write a letter for him home to East Livermore, Maine—I let him talk to me a little, but not much, advise him to keep very quiet—do most of the talking myself—stay quite a while with him, as he holds on to my hand—talk to him in a cheering, but slow, low, and measured manner—talk about his furlough, and going home as soon as he is able to travel.

3

Thomas Lindly, First Pennsylvania Cavalry, shot very badly through the foot—poor young man, he suffers horribly, has to be constantly dosed with morphine, his face ashy and glazed, bright young eyes—give him a large handsome apple, tell him to have it roasted in the mornii g, as he generally feels easier then, and can eat a little breakfast. I write two letters for him.

Opposite, an old Quaker lady is sitting by the side of her son, Amer Moore, Second U. S. Artillery—shot in the head two weeks since, very low, quite rational—from hips down, paralyzed—he will surely die. I speak a very few words to him every day and evening—he answers pleasantly—is a handsome fellow—wants nothing—(he told me soon after he came about his home affairs, his mother had been an invalid, and he fear'd to let her know his condition.) He died soon after she came.

(In my visits to the Hospitals I found it was in the simple matter of Personal Presence, and emanating ordinary cheer and magnetism, that I succeeded and help'd more than by medical nursing, or delicacies, or gifts of money, or anything else. During the war I possess'd the perfection of physical health. My habit, when practicable, was to prepare for starting out on one of those daily or nightly tours, of from a couple to four or five hours, by fortifying myself with previous rest, the bath, clean clothes, a good meal, and as cheerful an appearance as possible.)

June 25, (*Thursday, Sundown*).—As I sit writing this paragraph I see a train of about thirty huge four-horse wagons, used as ambulances, fill'd with wounded, passing up Fourteenth street, on their way, probably, to Columbian, Carver, and Mount Pleasant Hospitals. This is the way the men come in now, seldom in small numbers, but almost always in these long, sad processions. Through the past winter, while our army lay opposite Fredericksburgh, the like strings of ambulances were of frequent occurrence along Seventh street, passing slowly up from the steamboat wharf, with loads from Aquia Creek.

Bad Wounds, the Young.—The soldiers are nearly all young men, and far more American than is generally supposed—I should say nine-tenths are native-born. Among the arrivals from Chancellorsville I find a large proportion of Ohio, Indiana, and Illinois men. As usual, there are all sorts of wounds. Some of the men fearfully burnt from the explosion of artillery caissons. One Ward has a long row of officers, some with ugly hurts. Yesterday was perhaps worse than usual. Amputations are going on—the attendants are dressing wounds. As you pass by, you must be on your guard where you look. I saw the other day a gentleman, a visitor apparently from curiosity, in one of the Wards, stop and turn a moment to look at an awful wound they were probing, &c. He turn'd pale, and in a moment more he had fainted away and fallen on the floor.

June 29.—Just before sundown this evening a very large cavalry force went by—a fine sight. The men evidently had seen service. First came a mounted band of sixteen bugles, drums and cymbals, playing wild martial tunes—made my heart jump. Then the principal officers, then company after company, with their officers at their heads, making of course the main part of the cavalcade ; then a long train of men with led horses, lots of mounted negroes with special horses—and a long string of baggage-waggons, each drawn by four horses—and then a motley rear guard. It was a pronouncedly warlike and gay show. The sabres clank'd, the men look'd young and healthy and strong ; the electric tramping of so many horses on the hard road, and the gallant bearing, fine seat, and bright faced appearance of a thousand and more handsome young American men, were so good to see—quite set me up for hours.

An hour later another troop went by, smaller in numbers, perhaps three hundred men. They too look'd like serviceable men, campaigners used to field and fight.

July 3.—This forenoon, for more than an hour, again long strings of cavalry, several regiments, very fine men and horses, four or five abreast. I saw them in Fourteenth street, coming in town from north. Several hundred extra horses, some of the mares with colts, trotting along. (Appear'd to be a number of prisoners too.).........How inspiriting always the cavalry regiments ! Our men are generally well mounted, they ride well, feel good, are young, and gay on the saddle, their blankets in a roll behind them, their sabres clanking at their sides. This noise and movement and the tramp of many horses' hoofs has a curious effect upon one. The bugles play—presently you hear them afar off, deaden'd, mix'd with other noises.

Then just as they had all pass'd, a string of ambulances commenced from the other way, moving up Fourteenth street north, slowly wending along, bearing a large lot of wounded to the hospitals.

4th July—Battle of GETTYSBURG,—The weather to-day, upon the whole, is very fine, warm, but from a smart rain last night, fresh enough, and no dust, which is a great relief for this city. I saw the parade about noon, Pennsylvania avenue, from Fifteenth street down toward the Capitol. There were three regiments of infantry, (I suppose the ones doing patrol duty here,) two or three societies of Odd Fellows, a lot of children in barouches, and a squad of policemen. (It was a useless imposition upon the soldiers —they have work enough on their backs without piling the like of this.)

As I went down the Avenue, saw a big flaring placard on

the bulletin board of a newspaper office, announcing " Glorious Victory for the Union Army!" Meade had fought Lee at Gettysburgh, Pennsylvania, yesterday and day before, and repuls'd him most signally, taken 3,000 prisoners, &c. (I afterwards saw Meade's despatch, very modest, and a sort of order of the day from the President himself, quite religious, giving thanks to the Supreme, and calling on the people to do the same, &c.)

I walk'd on to Armory Hospital—took along with me several bottles of blackberry and cherry syrup, good and strong, but innocent. Went through several of the Wards, announc'd to the soldiers the news from Meade, and gave them all a good drink of the syrups with ice water, quite refreshing.........Meanwhile the Washington bells are ringing their sundown peals for Fourth of July, and the usual fusillades of boys' pistols, crackers, and guns.

A Cavalry Camp.—I am writing this nearly sundown, watching a Cavalry company, (acting Signal Service,) just come in through a shower, and making their night's camp ready on some broad, vacant ground, a sort of hill, in full view, opposite my window. There are the men in their yellow-striped jackets. All are dismounted; the freed horses stand with drooping heads and wet sides. They are to be led off presently in groups, to water. The little wall-tents and shelter-tents spring up quickly. I see the fires already blazing, and pots and kettles over them. The laggards among the men are driving in tent-poles, wielding their axes with strong, slow blows. I see great huddles of horses, bundles of hay, men, (some with unbuckled sabres yet on their sides,) a few officers, piles of wood, the flames of the fires, comrades by two and threes, saddles, harness, &c. The smoke streams upward, additional men arrive and dismount—some drive in stakes, and tie their horses to them ; some go with buckets for water, some are chopping wood, and so on.

July 6.—A steady rain, dark and thick and warm. A train of six-mule wagons has just pass'd bearing pontoons, great square-end flat-boats, and the heavy planking for overlaying them. We hear that the Potomac above here is flooded, and are wondering whether Lee will be able to get back across again, or whether Meade will indeed break him to pieces.

The cavalry camp on the hill is a ceaseless field of observation for me. This forenoon there stand the horses, huddled, tether'd together, dripping, steaming, chewing their hay. The men emerge from their tents, dripping also. The fires are half quench'd.

July 10.—Still the camp opposite—perhaps 50 or 60 tents. Some of the men are cleaning their sabres, (pleasant to-day,) some brushing boots, some laying off, reading, writing—some cooking, some sleeping—On long temporary cross-sticks back of the tents are hung saddles and cavalry accoutrements— blankets and overcoats are hung out to air—there are the squads of horses tether'd, feeding, continually stamping and whisking their tails to keep off flies.......I sit long in my third story window and look at the scene—a hundred little things going on—or peculiar objects connected with the camp that could not be described, any one of them justly, without much minute drawing and coloring in words.

A New York Soldier.—This afternoon, July 22, I have spent a long time with Oscar F. Wilber, Company G, One Hundred and Fifty-fourth New York, low with chronic diarrhœa, and a bad wound also. He ask'd me to read to him a chapter in the New Testament. I complied, and ask'd him what I should read. He said: " Make your own choice." I open'd at the close of one of the first books of the Evangelists, and read the chapters describing the latter hours of Christ, and the scenes at the crucifixion. The poor, wasted young man ask'd me to read the following chapter also, how Christ rose again. I read very slowly, for Oscar was feeble. It pleas'd him very much, yet the tears were in his eyes. He ask'd me if I enjoy'd religion. I said: " Perhaps not, my dear, in the way you mean, and yet, may-be, it is the same thing." He said: " It is my chief reliance." He talk'd of death, and said he did not fear it. I said : " Why, Oscar, don't you think you will get well?" He said: " I may, but it is not probable." He spoke calmly of his condition. The wound was very bad ; it discharg'd much. Then the diarrhœa had prostrated him, and I felt that he was even then the same as dying. He behaved very manly and affectionate. The kiss I gave him as I was about leaving he return'd fourfold. He gave me his mother's address, Mrs. Sally D. Wilber, Alleghany Post-office, Cattaraugus County, N. Y. I had several such interviews with him. He died a few days after the one just described.

Aug. 8.—To-night, as I was trying to keep cool, sitting by a wounded soldier in Armory Square, I was attracted by some pleasant singing in an adjoining Ward. As my soldier was asleep, I left him, and entering the Ward where the music was, I walk'd half way down and took a seat by the cot of a young Brooklyn friend, S. R., badly wounded in the hand at Chancellorsville, and who has suffer'd much, but who at that moment in the evening was wide awake and comparatively easy. He had turn'd over on his left side to get a better view of the singers, but the plentiful drapery of the musquito curtains of the adjoining cots obstructed the sight. I stept round and loop'd them all up, so that he had a clear show, and then sat down again by him, and look'd and listened. The principal singer was a young lady nurse of one of the Wards, accompanying on a melodeon, and join'd

by the lady nurses of other Wards. They sat there, making
a charming group, with their handsome, healthy faces ; and
standing up a little behind them were some ten or fifteen of
the convalescent soldiers, young men, nurses, &c., with
books in their hands, taking part in the singing. Of course
it was not such a performance as the great soloists at the
New York Opera House take a hand in ; but I am not sure
but I receiv'd as much pleasure, under the circumstances,
sitting there, as I have had from the best Italian compositions, express'd by world-famous performers.......The scene
was, indeed, an impressive one. The men lying up and down
the hospital, in their cots, (some badly wounded—some never
to rise thence,) the cots themselves, with their drapery of
white curtains, and the shadows down the lower and upper
parts of the Ward ; then the silence of the men, and the atti-
tudes they took—the whole was a sight to look around upon
again and again. And there, sweetly rose those female
voices up to the high, whitewash'd wooden roof, and pleasantly the roof sent it all back again. They sang very well ;
mostly quaint old songs and declamatory hymns, to fitting
tunes. Here, for instance, is one of the songs they sang:

SHINING SHORES.

My days are swiftly gliding by, and I a Pilgrim stranger,
Would not detain them as they fly, those hours of toil and danger ;
For O we stand on Jordan's strand, our friends are passing over,
And just before, the shining shores we may almost discover.

We'll gird our loins my brethren dear, our distant home discerning,
Our absent Lord has left us word, let every lamp be burning,
For O we stand on Jordan's strand, our friends are passing over,
And just before, the shining shores we may almost discover.

As the strains reverberated through the great edifice of
boards, (an excellent place for musical performers,) it was
plain to see how it all sooth'd and was grateful to the men.
I saw one near me turn over, and bury his face partially in
his pillow ; he was probably ashamed to be seen with wet
eyes.

Aug. 12.—I see the President almost every day, as I happen to live where he passes to or from his lodgings out of
town. He never sleeps at the White House during the hot
season, but has quarters at a healthy location, some three
miles north of the city, the Soldiers' Home, a United States
military establishment. I saw him this morning about 8½
coming in to business, riding on Vermont avenue, near L
street. The sight is a significant one, (and different enough
from how and where I first saw him.*) He always has a

---

* I shall not easily forget the first time I saw Abraham Lincoln. It must
have been about the 18th or 19th of February, 1861. It was rather a pleasant
spring afternoon, in New York city, as Lincoln arrived there from the West to
stop a few hours and then pass on to Washington, to prepare for his inauguration. I saw him in Broadway, near the site of the present Post-office. He had
come down, I think, from Canal street, to stop at the Astor House. The broad
spaces, sidewalks, and street in the neighborhood, and for some distance, were

company of twenty-five or thirty cavalry, with sabres drawn,
and held upright over their shoulders. The party makes no
great show in uniforms or horses. Mr. Lincoln, on the
saddle, generally rides a good-sized easy-going gray horse, is
dress'd in plain black, somewhat rusty and dusty; wears a
black stiff hat, and looks about as ordinary in attire, &c., as
the commonest man. A Lieutenant, with yellow straps,
rides at his left, and following behind, two by two, come the
cavalry men in their yellow-striped jackets. They are generally going at a slow trot, as that is the pace set them by
the One they wait upon. The sabres and accoutrements
clank, and the entirely unornamental *cortege* as it trots towards Lafayette square, arouses no sensation, only some
curious stranger stops and gazes. I see very plainly ABRA-
HAM LINCOLN'S dark brown face, with the deep cut lines,
the eyes, &c., always to me with a deep latent sadness in
the expression. We have got so that we always exchange
bows, and very cordial ones.

Sometimes the President goes and comes in an open
barouche. The cavalry always accompany him, with drawn
sabres. Often I notice as he goes out evenings—and sometimes in the morning, when he returns early—he turns off
and halts at the large and handsome residence of the Secretary of War, on K street, and holds conference there. If in
his barouche, I can see from my window he does not alight,
but sits in the vehicle, and Mr. Stanton comes out to attend
him. Sometimes one of his sons, a boy of ten or twelve,
accompanies him, riding at his right on a pony.

Earlier in the summer I occasionally saw the President

crowded with solid masses of people, many thousands. The omnibuses and
other vehicles had been all turn'd off, leaving an unusual hush in that busy
part of the city. Presently two or three shabby hack barouches made their
way with some difficulty through the crowd, and drew up at the Astor House
entrance. A tall figure step'd out of the centre of these barouches, paus'd
leisurely on the sidewalk, look'd up at the dark granite walls and looming
architecture of the grand old hotel—then, after a relieving stretch of arms and
legs, turn'd round for over a minute to slowly and good-humoredly scan the
appearance of the vast and silent crowds—and so, with very moderate pace,
and accompanied by a few unknown-looking persons, ascended the portico
steps.

The figure, the look, the gait, are distinctly impress'd upon me yet; the
unusual and uncouth height, the dress of complete black, the stovepipe hat
push'd back on the head, the dark-brown complexion, the seam'd and wrinkled
yet canny-looking face, the black, bushy head of hair, the disproportionately
long neck, and the hands held behind as he stood observing the people. All
was comparative and ominous silence. The new comer look'd with curiosity
upon that immense sea of faces, and the sea of faces return'd the look with
similar curiosity. In both there was a dash of something almost comical. Yet
there was much anxiety in certain quarters. Cautious persons had fear'd that
there would be some outbreak, some mark'd indignity or insult to the President elect on his passage through the city, for he possess'd no personal popularity in New York, and not much political. No such outbreak or insult, however, occurr'd. Only the silence of the crowd was very significant to those
who were accustom'd to the usual demonstrations of New York in wild,
tumultuous hurrahs—the deafening tumults of welcome, and the thunder-
shouts of pack'd myriads along the whole line of Broadway, receiving Hungarian Kossuth or Filibuster Walker.

and his wife, toward the latter part of the afternoon, out in a
barouche, on a pleasure ride through the city.   Mrs. Lincoln
was dress'd in complete black, with a long crape veil.   The
equipage is of the plainest kind, only two horses, and they
nothing extra.   They pass'd me once very close, and I saw
the President in the face fully, as they were moving slow,
and his look, though abstracted, happen'd to be directed
steadily in my eye.   He bow'd and smiled, but far beneath
his smile I noticed well the expression I have alluded to.
None of the artists or pictures have caught the deep, though
subtle and indirect expression of this man's face.   There is
something else there.   One of the great portrait painters of
two or three centuries ago is needed.

Heated term.—There has lately been much suffering here
from heat.   We have had it upon us now eleven days.   I
go around with an umbrella and a fan.   I saw two cases of
sun-stroke yesterday, one in Pennsylvania avenue, and another in Seventh street.   The City Railroad Company loses
some horses every day.   Yet Washington is having a livelier
August, and is probably putting in a more energetic and
satisfactory summer, than ever before during its existence.
There is probably more human electricity, more population
to make it, more business, more light-heartedness, than ever
before.   The armies that swiftly circumambiated from Fredericksburgh, march'd, struggled, fought, had out their mighty
clinch and hurl at Gettysburgh, wheel'd, have circumambiated again, return'd to their ways, touching us not, either at
their going or coming.   And Washington feels that she has
pass'd the worst; perhaps feels that she is henceforth mis-
tress.   So here she sits with her surrounding hills and shores
spotted with guns; and is conscious of a character and identity different from what it was five or six short weeks ago,
and very considerably pleasanter and prouder.

Soldiers and Talks.—Soldiers, soldiers, soldiers, you meet
everywhere about the city, often superb looking men, though
invalids dress'd in worn uniforms, and carrying canes or
crutches.   I often have talks with them, occasionally quite
long and interesting.   One, for instance, will have been all
through the Peninsula under McClellan—narrates to me
the fights, the marches, the strange, quick changes of that
eventful campaign, and gives glimpses of many things untold in any official reports or books or journals.   These, indeed, are the things that are genuine and precious.   The
man was there, has been out two years, has been through a
dozen fights, the superfluous flesh of talking is long work'd
off him, and now he gives me little but the hard meat and
sinew.......I find it refreshing, these hardy, bright, intuitive,
American young men, (experienced soldiers with all their
youth.)   The vital play and significance moves one more
than books.   Then there hangs something majestic about a

man who has borne his part in battles, especially if he is very quiet regarding it when you desire him to unbosom. I am continually lost at the absence of blowing and blowers among these old-young American militaires. I have found some man or another who has been in every battle since the War began, and have talk'd with them about each one, in every part of the United States, and many of the engagements on the rivers and harbors too. I find men here from every State in the Union, without exception. (There are more Southerners, especially Border State men, in the Union army than is generally supposed.) I now doubt whether one can get a fair idea of what this War practically is, or what genuine America is, and her character, without some such experience as this I am having.

Death of a Wisconsin Officer.—Another characteristic scene of that dark and bloody 1863, from notes of my visit to Armory Square Hospital, one hot but pleasant summer day. ....In Ward H we approach the cot of a young Lieutenant of one of the Wisconsin regiments. Tread the bare board floor lightly here, for the pain and panting of death are in this cot! I saw the Lieutenant when he was first brought here from Chancellorsville, and have been with him occasionally from day to day, and night to night. He had been getting along pretty well, till night before last, when a sudden hemorrhage that could not be stopt came upon him, and to-day it still continues at intervals. Notice that water-pail by the side of the bed, with a quantity of blood and bloody pieces of muslin—nearly full; that tells the story. The poor young man is lying panting, struggling painfully for breath, his great dark eyes with a glaze already upon them, and the choking faint but audible in his throat. An attendant sits by him, and will not leave him till the last; yet little or nothing can be done. He will die here in an hour or two without the presence of kith or kin. Meantime the ordinary chat and business of the Ward a little way off goes on indifferently. Some of the inmates are laughing and joking, others are playing checkers or cards, others are reading, &c. (I have noticed through most of the hospitals that as long as there is any chance for a man, no matter how bad he may be, the surgeon and nurses work hard, sometimes with curious tenacity, for his life, doing everything, and keeping somebody by him to execute the doctor's orders, and minister to him every minute night and day.........See that screen there. As you advance through the dusk of early candle-light, a nurse will step forth on tip-toe, and silently but imperiously forbid you to make any noise, or perhaps to come near at all. Some soldier's life is flickering there, suspended between recovery and death. Perhaps at this moment the exhausted frame has just fallen into a light sleep that a step might shake. You must retire. The neighboring patients

4

must move in their stocking feet. I have been several times struck with such mark'd efforts—everything bent to save a life from the very grip of the destroyer. But when that grip is once firmly fix'd, leaving no hope or chance at all, the surgeon abandons the patient. If it is a case where stimulus is any relief, the nurse gives milk-punch or brandy, or whatever is wanted, *ad libitum.* There is no fuss made. Not a bit of sentimentalism or whining have I seen about a single death-bed in hospital or on the field, but generally impassive indifference. All is over, as far as any efforts can avail; it is useless to expend emotions or labors. While there is a prospect they strive hard—at least most surgeons do; but death certain and evident, they yield the field.)

Aug., Sep., and Oct., '63—*The Hospitals.*—I am in the habit of going to all, and to Fairfax Seminary, Alexandria, and over Long Bridge to the great Convalescent Camp, &c. The journals publish a regular directory of them—a long list. As a specimen of almost any one of the larger of these Hospitals, fancy to yourself a space of three to twenty acres of ground, on which are group'd ten or twelve very large wooden barracks, with, perhaps, a dozen or twenty, and sometimes more than that number, of small buildings, capable altogether of accommodating from five hundred to a thousand or fifteen hundred persons. Sometimes these wooden barracks or Wards, each of them, perhaps, from a hundred to a hundred and fifty feet long, are ranged in a straight row, evenly fronting the street; others are plann'd so as to form an immense V; and others again are ranged around a hollow square. They make altogether a huge cluster, with the additional tents, extra wards for contagious diseases, guard-houses, sutler's stores, chaplain's house, &c. In the middle will probably be an edifice devoted to the offices of the Surgeon in Charge, and the Ward Surgeons, principal attaches, clerks, &c. Then around this centre radiate or are gather'd the Wards for the wounded and sick. The Wards are either letter'd alphabetically, Ward G, Ward K, or else numerically, 1, 2, 3, &c. Each has its Ward Surgeon and corps of nurses. Of course, there is, in the aggregate, quite a muster of employes, and over all the Surgeon in Charge.

The newspaper reader off through the agricultural regions, East or West, sees frequent allusions to these Hospitals, but has probably no clear idea of them. Here in Washington, when they are all fill'd, (as they have been already several times,) they contain a population more numerous in itself than the whole of the Washington of ten or fifteen years ago. Within sight of the Capitol, as I write, are some fifty or sixty such collections or camps, at times holding from fifty to seventy thousand men. Looking from any eminence and studying the topography in my rambles, I use them as landmarks. Through the rich August verdure of the trees see that white group of buildings off yonder in the outskirts; then another cluster half a mile to the left of the first; then another a mile to the right, and another a mile beyond, and still another between us and the first. Indeed, we can hardly look in any direction but these grim clusters are dotting the beautiful landscape and environs. That little town, as you might suppose it, off there on the brow of a hill, is indeed a town, but of wounds, sickness, and death. It .is Finley Hospital, northeast of the city, on Kendall Green, as it used to be call'd. That other is Campbell Hospital. Both are large establishments. I have known these two alone to have from two thousand to twenty-five hundred inmates. Then there is Carver Hospital, larger still, a wall'd and military city regularly laid out, and guarded by squads of sentries. Again, off east, Lincoln Hospital, a still larger one; and half a mile further Emory Hospital. Still sweeping the eye around down the river toward Alexandria, we see, to the right, the locality where the Conyalescent Camp stands, with its five, eight, or sometimes ten thousand inmates. Even all these are but a portion. The Harewood, Mount Pleasant, Armory Square, Judiciary Hospitals, are some of the rest, already mention'd, and all of them large collections.

Oct. 20.—To-night, after leaving the Hospital, at 10 o'cl'k, (I had been on self-imposed duty some five hours, pretty closely confined,) I wander'd a long time around Washington. The night was sweet, very clear, sufficiently cool, a voluptuous half-moon slightly golden, the space near it of a transparent tinge. I walk'd up Pennsylvania Avenue, and then to Seventh street, and a long while round the Patent Office. Somehow it look'd rebukefully strong, majestic, there in the delicate moonlight. The sky, the planets, the constellations all so bright, so calm, so expressively silent. so soothing, after those Hospital scenes. I wander'd to and fro till the moist moon set, long after midnight.

Spiritual Characters Among the Soldiers.—Every now and then in Hospital or Camp, there are beings I meet—specimens of unworldliness, disinterestedness and animal purity and heroism—perhaps some unconscious Indianian, or from Ohio or Tennessee—on whose birth the calmness of heaven seems to have descended, and whose gradual growing up, whatever the circumstances of work-life or change, or hardship, or small or no education that attended it, the power of a strange, spiritual sweetness, fibre and inward health have also attended. Something veil'd and abstracted is often a part of the manners of these beings. I have met them, I say, not seldom in the Army, in Camp, and in the great Hospitals. The Western regiments contain many of them. They are often young men, obeying the events and occasions about them, marching, soldiering, fighting, foraging, cooking, working on farms, or at some trade, before the war—unaware of their own nature, (as to that, who is aware of his own nature ?) their companions only understanding that they are different from the rest, more silent, "something odd about them," and apt to go off and meditate and muse in solitude.

Cattle Droves About Washington.—Among other sights are immense droves of cattle, with their drivers, passing through the streets of the city. Some of the men have a way of leading the cattle on by a peculiar call, a wild, pensive hoot, quite musical, prolong'd, indescribable, sounding something between the coo of a pigeon and the hoot of an owl. I like to stand and look at the sight of one of these immense droves—a little way off—(as the dust is great.) There are always men on horseback, cracking their whips and shouting—the cattle low—some obstinate ox or steer attempts to escape—then a lively scene—the mounted men, always excellent riders and on good horses, dash after the recusant, and wheel and turn—A dozen mounted drovers, their great, slouch'd, broad-brim'd hats, very picturesque—another dozen on foot—everybody cover'd with dust—long goads in their hands—An immense drove of perhaps 2000 cattle—the shouting, hooting, movement, &c.

Hospital Perplexity.—To add to other troubles, amid the confusion of this great army of sick, it is almost impossible for a stranger to find any friend or relative, unless he has the patient's address to start upon. Besides the directory printed in the newspapers here, there are one or two general directories of the Hospitals kept at Provost's headquarters, but they are nothing like complete; they are never up to date, and, as things are, with the daily streams of coming and going and changing, cannot be. (I have known cases, for instance, such as a farmer coming here from Northern New York to find a wounded brother, faithfully hunting round for a week, and then compell'd to leave and go home without getting any trace of him. When he got home he found a letter from the brother giving the right address in a hospital in Seventh street here.)

CULPEPPER, VA., *Feb.*, '64.—Here I am, pretty well down toward the extreme front. Three or four days ago General S., who is now in chief command, (I believe Meade is absent sick,) moved a strong force southward from camp as if intending business. They went to the Rapidan; there has since been some manouvering and a little fighting, but nothing of consequence. The telegraphic accounts given Monday morning last, make entirely too much of it, I should say. What General S. intended we here know not, but we trust in that competent commander. We were somewhat excited, (but not so very much either,) on Sunday, during the day and night, as orders were sent out to pack up and harness, and be ready to evacuate, to fall back toward Washington. I was very sleepy, and went to bed. Some tremendous shouts arousing me during the night, I went forth and found it was from the men above mention'd, who were returning. I talked with some of the men. As usual I found them full of gayety, endurance, and many fine little out-shows, the signs of the most excellent good manliness of the world.......It was a curious sight to see those shadowy columns moving through the night. I stood unobserv'd in the darkness and watch'd them long. The mud was very deep. The men had their usual burdens, overcoats, knapsacks, guns and blankets. Along and along they filed by me, with often a laugh, a song, a cheerful word, but never once a murmur. It may have been odd, but I never before so realized the majesty and reality of the American common people proper. It fell upon me like a great awe. The strong ranks moved neither fast nor slow. They had march'd seven or eight miles already through the slipping. unctious mud The brave First Corps stopt here. The equally brave Third Corps moved on to Brandy Station.

The famous Brooklyn 14th are here, guarding the town. You see their red legs actively moving everywhere. Then they have a theatre of their own here. They give musical performances, nearly every thing done capitally. Of course the audience is a jam. It is real good sport to attend one of these entertainments of the 14th. I like to look around at the soldiers, and the general collection of eager and handsome young faces in front of the curtain, more than the scene on the stage.

Paying the Bounties.—One of the things to note here now is the arrival of the paymaster with his strong box, and the payment of bounties to veterans re-enlisting. Major H. is here to-day, with a small mountain of greenbacks, rejoicing the hearts of the 2d division of the 1st Corps. In the midst of a ricketty shanty, behind a little table, sit the Major and Clerk Eldridge, with the rolls before them, and much moneys. A re-enlisted man gets in cash about $200 down, (and heavy instalments following, as the pay-days arrive, one after another.) The show of the men crowding around is quite exhilarating. I like well to stand and look. They feel elated, their pockets full, and the ensuing furlough, the visit home. It is a scene of sparkling eyes and flush'd cheeks. The soldier has many gloomy and harsh experiences, and this makes up for some of them. Major H. is order'd to pay first all the re-enlisted men of the 1st Corps their bounties and back pay, and then the rest. You hear the peculiar sound of the rustling of the new and crisp greenbacks by the hour, through the nimble fingers of the Major and my friend Clerk E.

Rumors, Changes, &c.—About the excitement of Sunday,

and the orders to be ready to start, I have heard since that
the said orders came from some cautious minor commander,
and that the high principalities knew not and thought not of
any such move; which is likely. The rumor and fear here
intimated a long circuit by Lee, and flank attack on our
right. But I cast my eyes at the mud, which was then at its
highest and palmiest condition, and retired composedly to
rest. Still it is about time for Culpepper to have a change.
Authorities have chased each other here like clouds in a
stormy sky. Before the first Bull Run this was the rendez-
vous and camp of instruction of the Secession troops. I am
stopping at the house of a lady who has witness'd all the
eventful changes of the War, along this route of contending
armies. She is a widow, with a family of young children,
and lives here with her sister in a large handsome house.
A number of army officers board with them.

Virginia.—Dilapidated, fenceless, and trodden with war as
Virginia is, wherever I move across her surface, I find myself rous'd to surprise and admiration. What capacity for
products, improvements, human life, nourishment and ex-
pansion! Everywhere that I have been in the Old Domin-
ion, (the subtle mockery of that title now!) such thoughts
have fill'd me. The soil is yet far above the average of any
of the northern States. And how full of breadth is the
scenery, everywhere with distant mountains, everywhere
convenient rivers. Even yet prodigal in forest woods, and
surely eligible for all the fruits, orchards, and flowers. The
skies and atmosphere most luscious, as I feel certain, from
more than a year's residence in the State, and movements
hither and yon. I should say very healthy, as a general
thing. Then a rich and elastic quality, by night and by day.
The sun rejoices in his strength, dazzling and burning, and
yet, to me, never unpleasantly weakening. It is not the
panting tropical heat, but invigorates. The north tempers
it. The nights are often unsurpassable. Last evening (Feb.
8,) I saw the first of the new moon, the old moon clear along
with it; the sky and air so clear, such transparent hues of
color, it seem'd to me I had never really seen the new moon
before. It was the thinnest cut crescent possible. It hung
delicate just above the sulky shadow of the Blue Mountains.
Ah, if it might prove an omen and good prophecy for this un-
happy State.

WASHINGTON *Again—Summer of* 1864.—I am back again
in Washington, on my regular daily and nightly rounds. Of
course there are many specialties. Dotting a Ward here and
there are always cases of poor fellows, long-suffering under
obstinate wounds, or weak and dishearten'd from typhoid
fever, or the like ; mark'd cases, needing special and sympa-
thetic nourishment. These I sit down and either talk to, or
silently cheer them up. They always like it hugely, (and so

do I.) Each case has its peculiarities, and needs some new adaptation. I have learnt to thus conform—learnt a good deal of hospital wisdom. Some of the poor young chaps, away from home for the first time in their lives, hunger and thirst for affection. This is sometimes the only thing that will reach their condition.......The men like to have a pencil, and something to write in. I have given them cheap pocket-diaries, and almanacs for 1864, interleav'd with blank paper. For reading I generally have some old pictorial magazines or story papers—they are always acceptable. Also the morning or evening papers of the day. The best books I do not give, but *lend* to read through the Wards, and then take them to others, and so on. They are very punctual about returning the books.

In these Wards, or on the field, as I thus continue to go round, I have come to adapt myself to each emergency, after its kind or call, however trivial, however solemn—every one justified and made real under its circumstances—not only visits and cheering talk and little gifts—not only washing and dressing wounds, (I have some cases where the patient is unwilling any one should do this but me)—but passages from the Bible, expounding them, prayer at the bed-side, explanations of doctrine, &c. (I think I see my friends smiling at this confession, but I was never more in earnest in my life.)

Readings.—In camp and everywhere, I was in the habit of reading to the men. They were very fond of it, and liked declamatory poetical pieces. We would gather in a large group by ourselves, after supper, and spend the time in such readings, or in talking, and occasionally by an amusing game called the Game of Twenty Questions.

A New Army Organization Fit for America Needed.—It is plain to me out of the events of the War, North and South, and out of all considerations, that the current Military theory, practice, rules and organization, (adopted from Europe from the feudal institutes, with, of course, the "modern improvements," largely from the French,) though tacitly follow'd, and believ'd in by the officers generally, are not at all consonant with the United States, nor our people, nor our days..... What it will be I know not—but I know that as entire an abnegation of the present Military System, (and the Naval too,) and a building up from radically different root-bases and centres appropriate to us, must eventually result, as that our Political system has resulted and become establish'd, different from feudal Europe, and built up on itself from original, perennial, democratic premises.

We have undoubtedly in the United States the greatest Military power—an exhaustless, intelligent, brave and reliable rank and file—in the world, any land, perhaps all lands. The problem is to organize this in the manner fully ap-

propriate to it, to the principles of the Republic, and to get
the best service out of it. In the present struggle, as already
seen and review'd, probably three-fourths of the losses, men,
lives, &c., have been sheer superfluity, extravagance,
waste. The body and bulk come out more and more superb—
the practical Military system, directing power, crude, illegiti-
mate—worse than deficient, offensive, radically wrong.

Death of a Hero.—I wonder if I could ever convey to another—to you, for instance, Reader dear—the tender and
terrible realities of such cases, (many, many happen'd,) as
the one I am now going to mention.......Stewart C. Glover,
Co. E, Fifth Wisconsin—was wounded, May 5, in one of those
fierce tussles of the Wilderness—died May 21—aged about
20. (He was a small and beardless young man—a splendid
soldier—in fact, almost an ideal American, of common life,
of his age. He had serv'd nearly three years, and would
have been entitled to his discharge in a few days. He was
in Hancock's Corps.).......The fighting had about ceas'd for
the day, and the General commanding the brigade rode by
and call'd for volunteers to bring in the wounded. Glover
responded among the first—went out gayly—but while in
the act of bearing in a wounded sergeant to our lines, was
shot in the knee by a rebel sharpshooter. Consequence,
amputation and death.......He had resided with his father,
John Glover, an aged and feeble man, in Batavia, Genesee
Co., N. Y., but was at school in Wisconsin, after the War
broke out, and there enlisted—soon took to soldier-life,
liked it, was very manly, was belov'd by officers and comrades.......He kept a little diary, like so many of the soldiers.
On the day of his death, he wrote the following in it : *To-
day, the doctor says I must die—all is over with me—ah, so
young to die.* On another blank leaf he pencill'd to his brother, *Dear brother Thomas, I have been brave, but wicked—pray
for me.*

A Slight Glimpse.—It is Sunday afternoon, middle of summer, hot and oppressive, and very silent through the Ward.
I am taking care of a critical case, now lying in a half lethargy. Near where I sit is a suffering rebel, from the Eighth
Louisiana ; his name is Irving. He has been here a long
time, badly wounded, and lately had his leg amputated. It
is not doing very well. Right opposite me is a sick soldier-
boy, laid down with his clothes on, sleeping, looking much
wasted, his pallid face on his arm. I see by the yellow
trimming on his jacket that he is a cavalry boy. He looks
so handsome as he sleeps, one must needs go nearer to him.
I step softly over and find by his card that he is named William Cone, of the First Maine Cavalry, and his folks live in
Skowhegan.

Ice Cream Treat.—One hot day toward the middle of June,
I gave the inmates of Carver Hospital a general ice cream

treat, purchasing a large quantity, and, under convoy of the doctor or head nurse of each Ward, going around personally through the Wards to see to its distribution.

An Incident.—In one of the fights before Atlanta, a rebel soldier, of large size, evidently a young man, was mortally wounded in top of the head, so that the brains partially exuded. He lived three days, lying on his back on the spot where he first dropt. He dug with his heel in the ground during that time a hole big enough to put in a couple of ordinary knapsacks. He just lay there in the open air, and with little intermission kept his heel going night and day. Some of our soldiers then moved him to a house, but he died in a few minutes.

Another.—After the battles at Columbia, Tennessee, where we repuls'd about a score of vehement rebel charges, they left a great many wounded on the ground, mostly within our range. Whenever any of these wounded attempted to move away by any means, generally by crawling off, our men without exception, brought them down by a bullet. They let none crawl away, no matter what his condition.

A Yankee Soldier.—As I turn'd off the Avenue one cool October evening into Thirteenth street, a soldier with knapsack and overcoat on, stood at the corner inquiring his way. I found he wanted to go part of the road in my direction, so we walk'd on together. We soon fell into conversation. He was small and not very young, and a tough little fellow, as I judged in the evening light, catching glimpses by the lamps we pass'd. His answers were short, but clear. His name was Charles Carroll; he belong'd to one of the Massachusetts regiments, and was born in or near Lynn. His parents were living, but were very old. There were four sons, and all had enlisted. Two had died of starvation and misery in the prison at Andersonville, and one had been kill'd in the West. He only was left. He was now going home, and, by the way he talk'd, I inferr'd that his time was nearly out. He made great calculations on being with his parents to comfort them the rest of their days.

Union Prisoners South—Salisbury.—Michael Stansbury, 48 years of age, a sea-faring man, a Southerner by birth and raising, formerly Captain of U. S. light ship Long Shoal, station'd at Long Shoal Point, Pamlico Sound—though a Southerner, a firm Union man—was captur'd Feb. 17, 1863, and has been nearly two years in the Confederate prisons; was at one time order'd releas'd by Governor Vance, but a rebel officer re-arrested him; then sent on to Richmond for exchange—but instead of being exchanged was sent down (as a Southern citizen, not a soldier,) to Salisbury, N. C., where he remain'd until lately, when he escaped among the exchanged by assuming the name of a dead soldier, and coming up via Wilmington with the rest. Was about

5

sixteen months in Salisbury. Subsequent to October '64, there were about 11,000 Union prisoners in the stockade ; about 100 of them Southern Unionists, 200 U. S. deserters. During the past winter 1500 of the prisoners, to save their lives, join'd the Confederacy, on condition of being assign'd merely to guard duty, &c. Out of the 11,000 not more than 2,500 came out ; 500 of these were pitiable, helpless wretches— the rest were in a condition to travel. There were often 60 dead bodies to be buried in the morning ; the daily average would be about 40. The regular food was a meal of corn, the cob and husk ground together, and sometimes once a week a ration of sorghum molasses. A diminutive ration of meat might possibly come once a month, not oftener....... In the stockade, containing the 11,000 men, there was a partial show of tents, (not enough for 2,000.) A large proportion of the men lived in holes in the ground, in the utmost wretchedness. Some froze to death, others had their hands and feet frozen. The rebel guards would occasionally, and on the least pretence, fire into the prison from mere demonism and wantonness. All the horrors that can be named, cruelty, starvation, lassitude, filth, vermin, despair, swift loss of self-respect, idiocy, insanity, and frequent murder, were there.......Stansbury has a wife and child living in Newbern—has written to them from here—is in the U. S. Light House employ still—(had been home to Newbern to see his family, and on his return to light ship was captured in his boat.).......Has seen men brought there to Salisbury as hearty as you ever see in your life—in a few weeks completely dead gone, much of it from thinking on their condition—hope all gone.......Has himself a hard, sad, strangely expressive, deaden'd kind of look, as of one chill'd for years in the cold and dark, where his good manly nature had no room to exercise itself.

Deserters—Saturday, Oct. 24.—Saw a large squad of our own deserters, (over 300) surrounded with a strong cordon of arm'd guards, marching along Pennsylvania avenue. The most motley collection I ever saw, all sorts of rig, all sorts of hats and caps, many fine-looking young fellows, some of them shame-faced, some sickly, most of them dirty, shirts very dirty and long worn, &c. They tramp'd along without order, a huge huddling mass, not in ranks. I saw some of the spectators laughing, but I felt like anything else but laughing.

These deserters are far more numerous than would be thought. Almost every day I see squads of them, sometimes two or three at a time, with a small guard; sometimes ten or twelve, under a larger one. (I hear that desertions from the army now in the field have often averaged 10,000 a month. One of the commonest sights in Washington is a squad of deserters. I often think it curious that the military and civil operations do not clash, but they never do here.)

A Glimpse of War's Hell-Scenes.—In one of the late movements of our troops in the Valley, (near Upperville, I think,) a strong force of Moseby's mounted guerillas attack'd a train of wounded, and the guard of cavalry convoying them. The ambulances contain'd about 60 wounded, quite a number of them officers of rank. The rebels were in strength, and the capture of the train and its partial guard after a short snap was effectually accomplish'd.

No sooner had our men surrender'd, the rebels instantly commenced robbing the train, and murdering their prisoners, even the wounded. Here is the scene, or a sample of it, ten minutes after. Among the wounded officers in the ambulances were one, a Lieutenant of regulars, and another of higher rank. These two were dragg'd out on the ground on their backs, and were now surrounded by the guerillas, a demoniac crowd, each member of which was stabbing them in different parts of their bodies. One of the officers had his feet pinn'd firmly to the ground by bayonets stuck through them and thrust into the ground. These two officers, as afterwards found on examination, had receiv'd about twenty such thrusts, some of them through the mouth, face, &c. The wounded had all been dragg'd (to give a better chance also for plunder,) out of their wagons; some had been effectually dispatch'd, and their bodies lying there lifeless and bloody. Others, not yet dead, but horribly mutilated, were moaning or groaning. Of our men who surrender'd, most had been thus maim'd or slaughter'd.

At this instant a force of our cavalry, who had been following the train at some interval, charged suddenly upon the Secesh captors, who proceeded at once to make the best escape they could. Most of them got away, but we gobbled two officers and seventeen men, as it were in the very acts just described. The sight was one which admitted of little discussion, as may be imagined. The seventeen captured men and two officers were put under guard for the night, but it was decided there and then that they should die.

The next morning the two officers were taken in the town, separate places, put in the centre of the street, and shot. The seventeen men were taken to an open ground, a little to one side. They were placed in a hollow square, encompass'd by two of our cavalry regiments, one of which regiments had three days before found the bloody corpses of three of their men hamstrung and hung up by the heels to limbs of trees by Moseby's guerillas, and the other had not long before had twelve men, after surrendering, shot and then hung by the neck to limbs of trees, and jeering inscriptions pinn'd to the breast of one of the corpses, who had been a sergeant. Those three, and those twelve, had been found, I say, by these environing regiments. Now, with revolvers, they form'd the grim cordon of their seventeen prisoners. The latter were placed in the midst of the hollow square, were unfasten'd, and the ironical remark made to them that they were now to be given "a chance for themselves." A few ran for it. But what use ? From every side the deadly pills came. In a few minutes the seventeen corpses strew'd the hollow square....... I was curious to know whether some of the Union soldiers, some few, (some one or two at least of the youngsters,) did not abstain from shooting on the helpless men. Not one. There was no exultation, very little said ; almost nothing, yet every man there contributed his shot.

(Multiply the above by scores, aye hundreds—varify it in all the forms that different circumstances, individuals, places, &c., could afford—light it with every lurid passion, the wolf's, the lion's lapping thirst for blood, the passionate, boiling volcanoes of human revenge for comrades, brothers slain— with the light of burning farms, and heaps of smutting, smouldering black embers—and in the human heart every- where black, worse embers—and you have an inkling of this War.)

Gifts—Money—Discrimination.—As a very large propor- tion of the wounded still come up from the front without a cent of money in their pockets, I soon discover'd that it was about the best thing I could do to raise their spirits, and show them that somebody cared for them, and practically felt a fatherly or brotherly interest in them, to give them small sums, in such cases, using tact and discretion about it. I am regularly supplied with funds for this purpose by good women and men in Boston, Salem, Providence, Brooklyn, and New York. I provide myself with a quantity of bright, new ten-cent and five-cent bills, and, when I think it incum- bent, I give 25 or 30 cents, or perhaps 50 cents, and occa- sionally a still larger sum to some particular case.

As I have recurr'd to this subject several times, I may take opportunity to ventilate and sum up the financial ques- tion. My supplies, altogether voluntary, mostly confiden- tial, often seeming quite Providential, were numerous and varied. For instance, there were two distant and wealthy ladies, sisters, who sent regularly, for two years. quite heavy sums, enjoining that their names should be kept secret. The same delicacy was indeed a frequent condition. From several I had *carte blanche.* Many were entire strangers. From these sources, during from two to three years, in the manner described, in the Hospitals, I bestow'd, as almoner for others, many, many thousands of dollars. I learn'd one thing conclusively—that beneath all the ostensible greed and heartlessness of our times there is no end to the gener- ous benevolence of men and women in the United States, when once sure of their object. Another thing became clear to me—while *cash* is not amiss to bring up the rear, tact and magnetic sympathy and unction are, and ever will be, sov- ereign still.

Items Wanted—(*From my Note Books.*)—Some of the half-erased and not over-legible when made, memoranda of things wanted, by one patient or another, will convey quite a fair idea. D. S. G. bed 52, wants a good book; has a sore, weak throat; would like some horehound candy. Is from New Jersey, 28th regiment.......C. H. L., 145th Pennsylvania, lies in bed 6, with jaundice and erysipelas; also wounded. Stomach easily nauseated. Bring him some oranges, also a little tart jelly. Hearty, full-blooded young fellow. (He got better in a few days, and is now home on a furlough.).......J. H. G., bed 24, wants an undershirt, drawers and socks. Has not had a change for quite a while. Is evidently a neat clean boy from New England. I supplied him; also with a comb, tooth-brush, and some soap and towels. I noticed afterward he was the cleanest of the whole Ward.......Mrs. G., lady nurse, Ward F., wants a bottle of brandy—has two patients imperatively requiring stimulus—low with wounds and exhaustion. (I supplied her with a bottle of first-rate brandy, from the Christian Commission rooms.)

A Case from Second Bull Run.—Well, poor John Mahay is dead. He died yesterday. His was a painful and long lingering case, (see p. 10, *ante*.) I have been with him at times for the past fifteen months. He belonged to Company A, One Hundred and First New York, and was shot through the lower region of the abdomen at second Bull Run, August, '62. One scene at his bedside will suffice for the agonies of nearly two years. The bladder had been perforated by a bullet going entirely through him. Not long since I sat a good part of the morning by his bedside, Ward E, Armory Square. The water ran out of his eyes from the intense pain, and the muscles of his face were distorted, but he utter'd nothing except a low groan now and then. Hot moist cloths were applied, and reliev'd him somewhat. Poor Mahay, a mere boy in age, but old in misfortune. He never knew the love of parents, was placed in his infancy in one of the New York charitable institutions, and subsequently bound out to a tyrannical master in Sullivan County, (the scars of whose cowhide and club remain'd yet on his back.) His wound here was a most disagreeable one, for he was a gentle, cleanly and affectionate boy. He found friends in his hospital life, and, indeed, was a universal favorite. He had quite a funeral ceremony.

Army Surgeons—Aid deficiencies.—I must bear my most emphatic testimony to the zeal, manliness, and professional spirit and capacity, generally prevailing among the Surgeons, many of them young men, in the Hospitals and the army. I will not say much about the exceptions, for they are few; (but I have met some of those few, and very incompetent and airish they were.) I never ceas'd to find the best young men, and the hardest and most disinterested workers, among these Surgeons, in the Hospitals. They are full of genius, too. I have seen many hundreds of them, and this is my testimony.

There are, however, serious deficiencies, wastes, sad want of system, &c., in the Commissions, contributions, and in all the Voluntary, and a great part of the Governmental, nursing, edibles, medicines, stores, &c. (I do not say surgical attendance, because the Surgeons cannot do more than human endurance permits.) Whatever puffing accounts there may be in the papers of the North, this is the actual fact. No thorough previous preparation, no system, no foresight, no genius. Always plenty of stores, no doubt, but always miles away ; never where they are needed, and never the proper application. Of all harrowing experiences, none is greater than that of the days following a heavy battle. Scores, hundreds of the noblest young men on earth, uncomplaining, lie, helpless, mangled, faint, alone, and so bleed to death, or die from exhaustion, either actually untouch'd at all, or merely the laying of them down and leaving them, when there ought to be means provided to save them.

The Blue everywhere.—This city, its suburbs, the Capitol, the front of the White House, the places of amusement, the Avenue, and all the main streets, swarm with soldiers this winter more than ever before. Some are out from the Hospitals, some from the neighboring camps, &c. One source or another, they pour in plenteously, and make, I should say, the mark'd feature in the human movement and costume-appearance of our National city. Their blue pants and overcoats are everywhere. The clump of crutches is heard, and up the stairs of the Paymasters' offices ; and there are characteristic groups around the doors of the same, often waiting long and wearily in the cold.......Toward the latter part of the afternoon you see the furlough'd men, sometimes singly, sometimes in small squads, making their way to the Baltimore depot. At all times, except early in the morning, the patrol detachments are moving around, especially during the earlier hours of evening, examining passes, and arresting all without them. They do not question the one-legged, or men badly disabled or maim'd, but all others are stopt. They also go around through the auditoriums of the theatres, and make officers and all show their passes, or other authority, for being there.

Sunday, Jan. 29, 1865.—Have been in Armory Square this afternoon. The Wards are very comfortable, with new floors and plaster walls, and models of neatness. I am not sure but this is a model hospital. after all, in important respects. I found several sad cases of old, lingering wounds. One Delaware soldier, Wm. H. Millis, from Bridgeville, whom I had been with after the battles of the Wilderness, last May, where he receiv'd a very bad wound in the chest, with another in the left arm, and whose case was serious (pneumonia had set in) all last June and July, I now find well enough to do light duty. For three weeks at the time mention'd, he just hover'd between life and death.

Boys in the Army.—As I walk'd home about sunset, I saw in Fourteenth street a very young soldier, thinly clad, standing near the house I was about to enter. I stopt a moment in front of the door and call'd him to me. I knew that an old Tennessee Union regiment, and also an Indiana regiment, were temporarily stopping in new barracks, near Fourteenth street. This boy I found belonged to the Tennessee regiment. But I could hardly believe he carried a musket. He was but 15 years old, yet had been twelve months a soldier, and had borne his part in several battles, even historic ones.......I ask'd him if he did not suffer from the cold and if he had no overcoat. No, he did not suffer from cold, and had no overcoat, but could draw one whenever he wish'd. His father was dead, and his mother living in some part of East Tennessee; all the men were from that part of the country.

The next forenoon I saw the Tennessee and Indiana regiments marching down the Avenue. My boy was with the former, stepping along with the rest. There were many other boys no older. I stood and watch'd them as they tramp'd along with slow, strong, heavy, regular steps. There did not appear to be a man over 30 years of age, and a large proportion were from 15 to perhaps 22 or 23. They had all the look of veterans, worn, stain'd, impassive, and a certain unbent, lounging gait, carrying in addition to their regular arms and knapsacks, frequently a frying-pan, broom, &c. They were all of pleasant, even handsome physiognomy; no refinement, nor blanch'd with intellect, but as my eye pick'd them, moving along, rank by rank, there did not seem to be a single repulsive, brutal or markedly stupid face among them.

Burial of a Lady Nurse.—Here is an incident that has just occurr'd in one of the Hospitals. A lady named Miss or Mrs. Billings, who has long been a practical friend of soldiers and nurse in the army, and had become attach'd to it in a way that no one can realize but him or her who has had experience, was taken sick, early this winter, linger'd some time, and finally died in the Hospital. It was her request that she should be buried among the soldiers, and after the military method. This request was fully carried out. Her coffin was carried to the grave by soldiers, with the usual escort, buried, and a salute fired over the grave. This was at Annapolis a few days since.

Female Nurses for Soldiers.—There are many women in one position or another, among the Hospitals, mostly as nurses here in Washington, and among the military stations;

quite a number of them young ladies acting as volunteers. They are a great help in certain ways, and deserve to be mention'd with praise and respect. Then it remains to be distinctly said that few or no young ladies, under the irresistible conventions of society, answer the practical requirements of nurses for soldiers. Middle-aged or healthy and good condition'd elderly women, mothers of children, are always best. Many of the wounded must be handled. A hundred things which cannot be gainsay'd, must occur and must be done. The presence of a good middle-aged or elderly woman, the magnetic touch of hands, the expressive features of the mother, the silent soothing of her presence, her words, her knowledge and privileges arrived at only through having had children, are precious and final qualifications. (Mrs. H. J. Wright, of Mansion House Hospital, Alexandria, is one of those good nurses. I have known her for over two years in her labors of love.) It is a natural faculty that is required; it is not merely having a genteel young woman at a table in a Ward. One of the finest nurses I met was a red-faced illiterate old Irish woman; I have seen her take the poor wasted naked boys so tenderly up in her arms. There are plenty of excellent clean old black women that would make tip-top nurses.

Southern Escapees, Feb. 23, '65.—I saw a large procession of young men from the rebel army, (deserters they are call'd, but the usual meaning of the word does not apply to them,) passing along the Avenue to-day. There were nearly 200 of them, come up yesterday by boat from James River. I stood and watch'd them as they pass'd along in a slow, tired, worn sort of way. There was a curiously large proportion of light-hair'd, blonde, light gray-eyed young men among them. Their costumes had a dirt-stain'd uniformity; most had been originally gray; some among them had articles of our uniform, pants on one, vest or coat on another. I think they were mostly Georgia and North Carolina boys. They excited little or no attention. As I stood quite close to them, several good looking enough American youths, (but O what a tale of misery their appearance told,) nodded or just spoke to me, without doubt divining pity and fatherliness out of my face, for my heart was full enough of it. Several of the couples trudged along with their arms about each other, some probably brothers; it seem'd as if they were afraid they might some how get separated. They nearly all look'd what one might call simple, yet intelligent enough, too. Some had pieces of old carpet, some blankets, and others old bags around their shoulders, and some of them here and there had fine faces, still it was a procession of misery. The two hundred had with them about half a dozen arm'd guards.

Along this week I saw some such procession, more or less

in numbers, every day, as they were brought up by the boat. The Government does what it can for them, and sends them North and West.

Feb. 27, '65.—Some three or four hundred more escapees from the Confederate army came up on the boat to-day. As the day has been very pleasant indeed, (after a long spell of bad weather,) I have been wandering around a good deal, without any other object than to be out-doors and enjoy it; have met these escaped men in all directions. Their apparel is the same ragged, long-worn motley as before described. I talk'd with a number of the men. Some are quite bright and stylish, for all their poor clothes—walking with an air, wearing their old head-coverings on one side, quite saucily. (I find the old, unquestionable proofs, as all along, the past four years, of the unscrupulous tyranny exercised by the Secession government in conscripting the common people by absolute force everywhere, and paying no attention whatever to the men's time being up—keeping them in military service just the same.).......One gigantic young fellow, a Georgian, at least six feet three inches high, broad-sized in proportion, attired in the dirtiest, drab, well-smear'd rags, his trousers at the knees all tied with strings, was complacently standing eating some bread and meat. He appear'd contented enough. Then a few minutes after I saw him slowly walking along. It was plain he did not take anything to heart.

Feb. 28.—As I pass'd the military headquarters of the city, not far from the President's house, I stopt to talk with some of the crowd of escapees who were lounging there. In appearance they were the same as previously mention'd. Two of them, one about 17, and the other perhaps 25 or 6, I talk'd with some time. They were from North Carolina, born and rais'd there, and had folks there. The elder had been in the rebel service four years. He was first conscripted for two years. He was then kept arbitrarily in the ranks. This is the case with a large proportion of the Secession army. There is no shame in leaving such service—was nothing downcast in these young men's manners. The younger had been soldiering about a year. He was conscripted. There were six brothers (all the boys of the family) in the army, part of them as conscripts, part as volunteers. Three had been kill'd. One had escaped about four months ago, and now this one had got away. He was a pleasant and well-talking lad, with the peculiar North Carolina idiom, (not at all disagreeable to my ears.) He and the elder one were of the same company, and escaped together—and wish'd to remain together. They thought of getting transportation away to Missouri, and working there; but were not sure it was judicious. I advised them rather to go to some of the directly northern States, and get farm work for the present

6

The younger had made six dollars on the boat, with some tobacco he brought ; he had three and a half left. The elder had nothing. I gave him a trifle.......Soon after, I met John Wormley, 9th Alabama—is a West Tennessee rais'd boy, parents both dead—had the look of one for a long time on short allowance—said very little—chew'd tobacco at a fearful rate, spitting in proportion—large clear dark-brown eyes, very fine—didn't know what to make of me—told me at last he wanted much to get some clean underclothes, and a pair of decent pants. Didn't care about coat or hat fixings. Wanted a chance to wash himself well, and put on the underclothes. I had the very great pleasure of helping him to accomplish all those wholesome designs.

March 1st.—Plenty more butternut or clay-color'd escapees every day. About 160 came in to-day, a large portion South Carolinians. They generally take the oath of allegiance, and are sent north, west, or extreme south-west if they wish. Several of them told me that the desertions in their army, of men going home, leave or no leave, are far more numerous than their desertions to our side. I saw a very forlorn looking squad of about a hundred, late this afternoon, on their way to the Baltimore depot.

To-night I have been wandering awhile in the Capitol, which is all lit up. The illuminated Rotunda looks fine. I like to stand aside and look a long, long while, up at the dome ; it comforts me somehow. The House and Senate were both in session till very late. I look'd in upon them, but only a few moments ; they were hard at work on tax and appropriation bills. I wander'd through the long and rich corridors and apartments under the Senate ; an old habit of mine, former winters, and now more satisfaction than ever. Not many persons down there, occasionally a flitting figure in the distance.

The Inauguration, March 4.—The President very quietly rode down to the Capitol in his own carriage, by himself, on a sharp trot, about noon, either because he wish'd to be on hand to sign bills, &c., or to get rid of marching in line with the absurd procession, the muslin Temple of Liberty, and pasteboard Monitor. I saw him on his return, at three o'clock, after the performance was over. He was in his plain two-horse barouche, and look'd very much worn and tired ; the lines, indeed, of vast responsibilites, intricate questions, and demands of life and death, cut deeper than ever upon his dark brown face ; yet all the old goodness, tenderness, sadness, and canny shrewdness, underneath the furrows. (I never see that man without feeling that he is one to become personally attach'd to, for his combination of purest, heartiest tenderness, and native Western even rudest forms of manliness.) By his side sat his little boy, of ten years. There were no soldiers, only a lot of civilians on horseback, with huge yellow scarfs over their shoulders, riding around the carriage. (At the Inauguration four years ago, he rode down and back again, surrounded by a dense mass of arm'd cavalrymen eight deep, with drawn sabres ; and there were sharp-shooters station'd at every corner on the route.)

I ought to make mention of the closing Levee of Saturday night last. Never before was such a compact jam in front of the White House—all the grounds fill'd, and away out to the spacious sidewalks.......I was there, as I took a notion to go—was in the rush inside with the crowd—surged along the passage-ways, the Blue and other rooms, and through the great East room, (upholster'd like a stage parlor.) Crowds of country people, some very funny. Fine music from the Marine Band, off in a side place.......I saw Mr. Lincoln, drest all in black, with white kid gloves, and a claw-hammer coat, receiving, as in duty bound, shaking hands, looking very disconsolate, and as if he would give anything to be somewhere else.

The Weather—Does it Sympathise with these Times?— Whether the rains, the heat and cold, and what underlies them all, are affected with what affects man in masses, and follow his play of passionate action, strain'd stronger than usual, and on a larger scale than usual—whether this, or no, it is certain that there is now, and has been for twenty months or more on this American Continent North, many a remarkable, many an unprecedented expression of the subtile world of air above us and around us. There, since this War, and the wide and deep National agitation, strange analogies, different combinations, a different sunlight, or absence of it ; different products even out of the ground. After every great battle, a great storm. Even civic events, the same. On Saturday last, a forenoon like whirling demons, dark, with slanting rain, full of rage ; and then the afternoon, so calm, so bathed with flooding splendor from heaven's most excellent sun, with atmosphere of sweetness ; so clear, it show'd the stars, long, long before they were due. As the President came out on the Capitol portico, a curious little white cloud, the only one in that part of the sky, appear'd like a hovering bird, right over him.

Indeed, the heavens, the elements, all the meteorological influences, have run riot for weeks past. Such caprices, abruptest alternation of frowns and beauty, I never knew. It is a common remark that (as last Summer was different in its spells of intense heat from any preceding it,) the Winter just completed has been without parallel. It has remain'd so down to the hour I am writing. Much of the daytime of the past month was sulky, with leaden heaviness, fog, interstices of bitter cold, and some insane storms. But there have been samples of another description. Nor earth, nor sky ever knew spectacles of superber beauty than some of the nights have lately been here. The western star, Venus, in the earlier hours of evening, has never been so large, so clear; it seems as if it told something, as if it held rapport indulgent with humanity, with us Americans. Five or six nights since, it hung close by the moon, then a little past its first quarter. The star was wonderful, the moon like a young mother. The sky, dark blue, the transparent night, the planets, the moderate west wind, the elastic temperature, the unsurpassable miracle of that great star, and the young and swelling moon swimming in the west, suffused the soul. Then I heard, slow and clear, the deliberate notes of a bugle come up out of the silence, sounding so good through the night's mystery, no hurry, but firm and faithful, floating along, rising, falling leisurely, with here and there a long-drawn note ; the bugle, well play'd, sounding tattoo, in one of the army Hospitals near here, where the wounded (some of them personally so dear to me,) are lying in their cots, and many a sick boy come down to the war from Illinois, Michigan, Wisconsin, Iowa, and the rest.

March 6—Inauguration Ball.—I have this moment been up to look at the gorgeous array'd dance and supper-rooms, for the Inauguration Ball, at the Patent Office, (which begins in a few hours ;) and I could not help thinking of those rooms, where the music will sound and the dancers' feet presently tread—what a different scene they presented to my view a while since, fill'd with a crowded mass of the worst wounded of the war, brought in from Second Bull Run, Antietam and Fredericksburgh. To-night, beautiful women, perfumes, the violins' sweetness, the polka and the waltz; but then, the amputation, the blue face, the groan, the glassy eye of the dying, the clotted rag, the odor of wounds and blood, and many a mother's son amid strangers, passing away untended there, (for the crowd of the badly hurt was great, and much for nurse to do, and much for surgeon.)

Scene at the Capitol.—I must mention a strange scene at the Capitol, the Hall of Representatives, the morning of Saturday last, (March 4th.) The day just dawn'd, but in half-darkness, everything dim, leaden, and soaking. In that dim light the members nervous from long drawn duty, exhausted, some asleep, and many half asleep. The gas-light, mix'd with the dingy day-break, produced an unearthly effect. The poor little sleepy, stumbling pages, the smell of the Hall, the members with heads leaning on their desks asleep, the sounds of the voices speaking, with unusual intonations—the general moral atmosphere also of the close of this important session—the strong hope that the War is approaching its close—the tantalizing dread lest the hope may be a false one—the grandeur of the Hall itself, with its effect of vast shadows up toward the panels and spaces over the galleries—all made a mark'd combination.

In the midst of this, with the suddenness of a thunderbolt, burst one of the most angry and crashing storms of rain and wind ever heard. It beat like a deluge on the heavy glass roof of the Hall, and the wind literally howl'd and roar'd. For a moment, (and no wonder,) the nervous and sleeping Representatives were thrown into confusion. The slumberers awaked with fear, some started for the doors, some look'd up with blanch'd cheeks and lips to the roof, and the little pages began to cry ; it was a scene ! But it was over almost as soon as the drowsied men were actually awake. They recover'd themselves ; the storm raged on, beating, dashing, and with loud noises at times. But the House went ahead with its business then, I think, as calmly and with as much deliberation as at any time in its career. Perhaps the shock did it good. (One is not without impression, after all, amid these members of Congress, of both the Houses, that if the flat and selfish routine of their duties should ever be broken in upon by some great emergency involving real danger, and calling for first-class personal qualities, those qualities would be found generally forthcoming, and from men not now credited with them.)

March 27, 1865—*A Yankee Antique.*—Sergeant Calvin F. Harlowe, Co. C, Twenty-Ninth Massachusetts, Third Brigade, First Division, Ninth Corps—a mark'd sample of heroism and death, (some may say bravado, but I say *heroism,* of grandest, oldest order)—in the late attack by the rebel troops, and temporary capture by them, of Fort Steadman, at night. The Fort was surprised at dead of night. Suddenly awaken'd from their sleep, and rushing from their tents. Harlowe, with others, found himself in the hands of the Secesh—they demanded his surrender—he answer'd, *Never while I live.* (Of course it was useless. The others surrender'd ; the odds were too great.) Again he was ask'd to yield, this time by a rebel Captain. Though surrounded, and quite calm, he again refused, call'd sternly to his comrades to fight on, and himself attempted to do so. The rebel Captain then shot him—but at the same instant he shot the Captain. Both fell together, mortally wounded. Harlowe died almost instantly. (The rebels were driven out in a very short time.) The body was buried next day, but soon taken up and sent home, (Plymouth Co., Mass.).......Harlowe was only 22 years of age—was a tall, slim, dark-hair'd, blue-eyed young man—had come out originally with the Twenty-Ninth Mass., and that is the way he met his death, after four years campaign. He was in the Seven Days Fight before Richmond, in Second Bull Run, Antietam, First Fredericksburgh, Vicksburgh, Jackson, Wilderness, and the campaigns following—was as good a soldier as ever wore the blue, and every old officer of the regiment will bear that testimony. ....Though so young, and in a common rank, he had a spirit as resolute and brave as any hero in the books, ancient or

modern—It was too great to say the words "I surrender"—
and so he died.......(When I think of such things, knowing
them well, all the vast and complicated events of the War
on which History dwells and makes its volumes, fall indeed
aside, and for the moment at any rate I see nothing but
young Calvin Harlowe's figure in the night disdaining to
surrender.)

Wounds and Diseases.—The war is over, but the hospitals
are fuller than ever, from former and current cases. A
large majority of the wounds are in the arms and legs. But
there is every kind of wound, in every part of the body. I
should say of the sick, from my observation, that the prevailing maladies are typhoid fever and the camp fevers generally, diarrhœa, catarrhal affections and bronchitis, rheuma-
tism and pneumonia. These forms of sickness lead; all the
rest follow. There are twice as many sick as there are
wounded. The deaths range from 7 to 10 per cent. of those
under treatment.

Murder of President Lincoln.—The day, April 14, 1865,
seems to have been a pleasant one throughout the whole
land—the moral atmosphere pleasant too—the long storm,
so dark, so fratricidal, full of blood and doubt and gloom,
over and ended at last by the sun-rise of such an absolute
National victory, and utter breaking-down of Secessionism—
we almost doubted our own senses! Lee had capitulated
beneath the apple-tree of Appomattax. The other armies,
the flanges of the revolt, swiftly follow'd.......And could
it really be, then? Out of all the affairs of this world of
woe and passion, of failure and disorder and dismay, was
there really come the confirm'd, unerring sign of plan, like
a shaft of pure light—of rightful rule—of God?.......So the
day, as I say, was propitious. Early herbage, early flowers,
were out. (I remember where I was stopping at the time,
the season being advanced, there were many lilacs in full
bloom. By one of those caprices that enter and give tinge
to events without being at all a part of them, I find myself
always reminded of the great tragedy of that day by the
sight and odor of these blossoms. It never fails.)

But I must not dwell on accessories. The deed hastens.
The popular afternoon paper of Washington, the little
Evening Star, had spatter'd all over its third page, divided
among the advertisements in a sensational manner in a hundred different places, *The President and his Lady will be at
the Theatre this evening*.......(Lincoln was fond of the theatre.
I have myself seen him there several times. I remember
thinking how funny it was that He, in some respects, the
leading actor in the greatest and stormiest drama known to
real history's stage, through centuries, should sit there and
be so completely interested and absorb'd in those human
jack-straws, moving about with their silly little gestures,
foreign spirit, and flatulent text.)

On this occasion the theatre was crowded, many ladies in rich and gay costumes, officers in their uniforms, many well known citizens, young folks, the usual clusters of gas-lights, the usual magnetism of so many people, cheerful, with perfumes, music of violins and flutes—(and over all, and saturating all, that vast vague wonder, *Victory*, the Nation's Victory, the triumph of the Union, filling the air, the thought, the sense, with exhilaration more than all perfumes.)

The President came betimes, and, with his wife, witness'd the play, from the large stage-boxes of the second tier, two thrown into one, and profusely draped with the National flag. The acts and scenes of the piece—one of those singularly written compositions which have at least the merit of giving entire relief to an audience engaged in mental action or business excitements and cares during the day, as it makes not the slightest call on either the moral, emotional, esthetic, or spiritual nature—a piece, ('Our American Cousin,') in which, among other characters, so call'd, a Yankee, certainly such a one as was never seen, or the least like it ever seen, in North America, is introduced in England, with a varied fol-de-rol of talk, plot, scenery, and such phantasmagoria as goes to make up a modern popular drama—had progress'd through perhaps a couple of its acts, when in the midst of this comedy, or tragedy, or non-such, or whatever it is to be call'd, and to off-set it or finish it out, as if in Nature's and the Great Muse's mockery of those poor mimes, comes interpolated that Scene, not really or exactly to be described at all, (for on the many hundreds who were there it seems to this hour to have left little but a passing blur, a dream, a blotch)—and yet partially to be described as I now proceed to give it.......There is a scene in the play representing a modern parlor, in which two unprecedented English ladies are inform'd by the unprecedented and impossible Yankee that he is not a man of fortune, and therefore undesirable for marriage-catching purposes; after which, the comments being finish'd, the dramatic trio make exit, leaving the stage clear for a moment. There was a pause, a hush as it were. At this period came the murder of Abraham Lincoln. Great as that was, with all its manifold train, circling round it, and stretching into the future for many a century, in the politics, history, art, &c., of the New World, in point of fact the main thing, the actual murder, transpired with the quiet and simplicity of any commonest occurrence—the bursting of a bud or pod in the growth of vegetation, for instance. Through the general hum following the stage pause, with the change of positions, &c., came the muffled sound of a pistol shot, which not one hundredth part of the audience heard at the time—and yet a moment's hush—somehow, surely a vague startled thrill—and then, through the ornamented, draperied, starr'd and striped space-way of the President's box, a sudden figure, a man raises himself with hands and feet, stands a moment on the railing, leaps below to the stage, (a distance of perhaps fourteen or fifteen feet,) falls out of position, catching his boot-heel in the copious drapery, (the American flag,) falls on one knee, quickly recovers himself, rises as if nothing had happen'd, (he really sprains his ankle, but unfelt then,)—and so the figure, Booth, the murderer, dress'd in plain black broadcloth, bare-headed, with a full head of glossy, raven hair, and his eyes like some mad animal's flashing with light and resolution, yet with a certain strange calmness, holds aloft in one hand a large knife—walks along not much back from the footlights—turns fully toward the audience his face of statuesque beauty, lit by those basilisk eyes, flashing with desperation, perhaps insanity—launches out in a firm and steady voice the words, *Sic semper tyrannis*—and then walks with neither slow nor very rapid pace diagonally across to the back of the stage, and disappears.......(Had not all this terrible scene—making the mimic ones preposterous—had it not all been rehears'd, in blank, by Booth, beforehand?)

A moment's hush, incredulous—a scream—the cry of *Murder*—Mrs. Lincoln leaning out of the box, with ashy cheeks and lips, with involuntary cry, pointing to the retreating figure, *He has kill'd the President*.......And still a moment's strange, incredulous suspense—and then the deluge!—then that mixture of horror, noises, uncertainty—(the sound, somewhere back, of a horse's hoofs clattering with speed)—the people burst through chairs and railings, and break them up—that noise adds to the queerness of the scene—there is inextricable confusion and terror—women faint—quite feeble persons fall, and are trampled on—many cries of agony are heard—the broad stage suddenly fills to suffocation with a dense and motley crowd, like some horrible carnival—the audience rush generally upon it—at least the strong men do—the actors and actresses are all there in their play-costumes and painted faces, with mortal fright showing through the rouge, some trembling—some in tears—the screams and calls, confused talk—redoubled, trebled—two or three manage to pass up water from the stage to the President's box—others try to clamber up—&c., &c., &c.

In the midst of all this, the soldiers of the President's Guard, with others, suddenly drawn to the scene, burst in—(some two hundred altogether)—they storm the house, through all the tiers, especially the upper ones, inflamed with fury, literally charging the audience with fix'd bayonets, muskets and pistols, shouting *Clear out! clear out! you sons of*——.......Such the wild scene, or a suggestion of it rather, inside the play-house that night.

Outside, too, in the atmosphere of shock and craze, crowds

of people, fill'd with frenzy, ready to seize any outlet for it, come near committing murder several times on innocent individuals. One such case was especially exciting. The infuriated crowd, through some chance, got started against one man, either for words he utter'd, or perhaps without any cause at all, and were proceeding at once to actually hang him on a neighboring lamp post, when he was rescued by a few heroic policemen, who placed him in their midst and fought their way slowly and amid great peril toward the Station House.......It was a fitting episode of the whole affair. The crowd rushing and eddying to and fro—the night, the yells, the pale faces, many frighten'd people trying in vain to extricate themselves—the attack'd man, not yet freed from the jaws of death, looking like a corpse—the silent resolute half-dozen policemen, with no weapons but their little clubs, yet stern and steady through all those eddying swarms—made indeed a fitting side-scene to the grand tragedy of the murder.......They gain'd the Station House with the protected man, whom they placed in security for the night, and discharged him in the morning.

And in the midst of that night-pandemonium of senseless hate, infuriated soldiers, the audience and the crowd—the stage, and all its actors and actresses, its paint-pots, spangles, and gas-lights—the life-blood from those veins, the best and sweetest of the land, drips slowly down, and death's ooze already begins its little bubbles on the lips.......Such, hurriedly sketch'd, were the accompaniments of the death of President Lincoln. So suddenly and in murder and horror unsurpass'd he *was* taken from us. But his death was painless.

[He leaves for America's History and Biography, so far, not only its most dramatic reminiscence—he leaves, in my opinion, the greatest, best, most characteristic, artistic, Personality. Not but that he had faults, and show'd them in the Presidency ; but honesty, goodness, shrewdness, conscience, and (a new virtue, unknown to other lands, and hardly yet really known here, but the foundation and tie of all, as the future will grandly develop,) Unionism, in its truest and amplest sense, form'd the hard-pan of his character. These he seal'd with his life. The tragic splendor of his death, purging, illuminating all, throws round his form, his head, an aureole that will remain and will grow brighter through time, while History lives, and love of Country lasts. By many has *this Union* been conserv'd and help'd ; but if one name, one man, must be pick'd out, he, most of all, is the Conservator of it, to the future. He was assassinated— but the Union is not assassinated—*ça ira !* One falls, and another falls. The soldier drops, sinks like a wave—but the ranks of the ocean eternally press on. Death does its work, obliterates a hundred, a thousand—President, general, captain, private—but the Nation is immortal.]

7

Releas'd Union Prisoners from South.—The releas'd prisoners of War are now coming up from the Southern prisons. I have seen a number of them. The sight is worse than any sight of battle-fields or any collections of wounded, even the bloodiest. There was, (as a sample,) one large boat load, of several hundreds, brought about the 25th, to Annapolis ; and out of the whole number only three individuals were able to walk from the boat. The rest were carried ashore and laid down in one place or another. Can those be *men*—those little livid-brown, ash-streak'd, monkey-looking dwarfs ?—are they really not mummied, dwindled corpses ? They lay there, most of them, quite still, but with a horrible look in their eyes and skinny lips, often with not enough flesh on the lips to cover their teeth. Probably no more appaling sight was ever seen on this earth. (There are deeds, crimes, that may be forgiven ; but this is not among them. It steeps its perpetrators in blackest, escapeless, endless damnation. Over 50,000 have been compell'd to die the death of starvation—reader, did you ever try to realize what *starvation* actually is ?—in those prisons—and in a land of plenty !)

An indescribable meanness, tyranny, aggravating course of insults, almost incredible—was evidently the rule of treatment through all the Southern military prisons. The dead there are not to be pitied as much as some of the living that come from there—if they can be call'd living—many of them are mentally imbecile, and will never recuperate.

Death of a Pennsylvania Soldier—Frank H. Irwin, Co. E, 93rd Pennsylvania—Died May 1, '65—My letter to his mother.— Dear Madam : No doubt you and Frank's friends have heard the sad fact of his death in Hospital here, through his uncle, or the lady from Baltimore, who took his things. (I have not seen them, only heard of them visiting Frank.) I will write you a few lines—as a casual friend that sat by his death bed.

Your son, Corporal Frank H. Irwin, was wounded near Fort Fisher, Virginia, March 25th, 1865—the wound was in the left knee, pretty bad. He was sent up to Washington, was receiv'd in Ward C, Armory Square Hospital, March 28th—the wound became worse, and on the 4th of April the leg was amputated a little above the knee—the operation was perform'd by Dr. Bliss, one of the best surgeons in the army—he did the whole operation himself—there was a good deal of bad matter gather'd—the bullet was found in the knee. For a couple of weeks afterwards he was doing pretty well. I visited and sat by him frequently, as he was fond of having me. The last ten or twelve days of April I saw that his case was critical. He previously had some fever, with cold spells. The last week in April he was much of the time flighty—but always mild and gentle. He died first of May. The actual cause of death was Pyæmia, (the absorption of the matter in the system instead of its discharge.)

Frank, as far as I saw, had everything requisite in surgical treatment, nursing, &c. He had watches much of the time. He was so good and well-behaved, and affectionate, I myself liked him very much. I was in the habit of coming in afternoons and sitting by him, and soothing him, and he liked to have me—liked to put his arm out and lay his hand on my knee—would keep it so a long while. Toward the last he was more restless and flighty at night —often fancied himself with his regiment—by his talk sometimes seem'd as if his feelings were hurt by being blamed by his officers for something he was entirely innocent of—said, "I never in my life was thought capable of such a thing, and never was." At other times he would fancy himself talking as it seem'd to children or such like, his relatives I suppose, and giving them good advice; would talk to them a long while. All the time he was out of his head not one single bad word or thought or idea escaped him. It was remark'd that many a man's conversation in his senses was not half as good as Frank's delirium.

He was perfectly willing to die—he had become very weak and had suffer'd a good deal, and was perfectly resign'd, poor boy. I do not know his past life, but I feel as if it must have been good. At any rate what I saw of him here, under the most trying circumstances, with a painful wound, and among strangers, I can say that he behaved so brave, so composed, and so sweet and affectionate, it could not be surpass'd. And now like many other noble and good men, after serving his country as a soldier, he has yielded up his young life at the very outset in her service. Such things are gloomy—yet there is a text, "God doeth all things well,"— the meaning of which, after due time, appears to the soul.

I thought perhaps a few words, though from a stranger, about your son, from one who was with him at the last, might be worth while, for I loved the young man, though I but saw him immediately to lose him. I am merely a friend visiting the Hospitals occasionally to cheer the wounded and sick. W. W.

May 7—(*Sunday.*)—To-day as I was walking a mile or two south of Alexandria, I fell in with several large squads of the returning Western Army, (*Sherman's men* as they call'd themselves) about a thousand in all, the largest portion of them half sick, some convalescents, &c. These fragmentary excerpts, with the unmistakable western physiognomy and idioms, crawling along slowly—after a great campaign, blown this way, as it were, out of their latitude—I mark'd with curiosity, and talk'd with off and on for over an hour. Here and there was one very sick; but all were able to walk, except some of the last, who had given out, and were seated on the ground, faint and despondent. These I tried to cheer, told them the camp they were to reach, (a sort of half-hospital,) was only a little way further over the hill, and so got them up and started on, accompanying some of the worst a little way, and helping them, or putting them under the support of stronger comrades.

May 21.—Saw General Sheridan and his Cavalry to-day. It was a strong, attractive, serious sight. We have been having rainy weather. The men were mostly young, (a few middle-aged,) superb-looking fellows, brown, spare, keen, with well-worn clothing, many with pieces of water-proof cloth around their shoulders and hanging down. They dash'd along pretty fast, in wide close ranks, all spatter'd with mud ; no holiday soldiers. Quite all Americans (The Americans are the handsomest race that ever trod the earth.) They came clattering along, brigade after brigade. I could have watch'd for a week. Sheridan stood on a balcony, under a big tree, coolly smoking a cigar. His looks and manner impress'd me favorably.

May 22.—Have been taking a walk along Pennsylvania Avenue and Seventh street north. The city is full of soldiers, running around loose. Officers everywhere, of all grades. All have the weather-beaten look of practical service. It is a sight I never tire of. All the Armies are now here (or portions of them,) for to-morrow's Review. You see them swarming like bees everywhere.

The Grand Review.—For two days now the broad spaces of Pennsylvania Avenue along to Treasury Hill, and so by detour around to the President's House, (and so up to Georgetown, and across the Aqueduct bridge,) have been alive with a magnificent sight, the returning Armies. In their wide ranks stretching clear across the Avenue I watch them march or ride along, at a brisk pace, through two whole days—Infantry, Cavalry, Artillery—some 200,000 men.........
Some days afterwards one or two other Corps.......and then, still afterwards, a good part of Sherman's immense Army, brought up from Charleston, Savannah, &c.

Western Soldiers—May 26–7.—The streets, the public buildings and grounds of Washington still swarm with soldiers from Illinois, Indiana, Ohio, Missouri, Iowa, and all the Western States. I am continually meeting and talking with them. They often speak to me first, and always show great sociability, and glad to have a good interchange of chat.......These Western soldiers are more slow in their movements, and in their intellectual quality also ; have no extreme alertness. They are larger in size, have a more serious physiognomy, are continually looking at you as they pass in the street. They are largely animal, and handsomely so. (During the War I have been at times with the Fourteenth, Fifteenth, Seventeenth, and Twentieth Corps.) I

always feel drawn toward the men, and like their personal
contact when we are crowded close together, as frequently
these days in the street-cars. They all think the world of
General Sherman ; call him "Old Bill," or sometimes
"Uncle Billy."

May 28.—As I sat by the bedside of a sick Michigan soldier in a Hospital to-day, a convalescent from the adjoining
bed rose and came to me, and presently we began talking.
He was a middle-aged man, belonged to the 2d Virginia
regiment, but lived in Racine, Ohio, and had a family there.
He spoke of President Lincoln, and said : " The war is over,
and many are lost. And now we have lost the best, the
fairest, the truest man in America. Take him altogether
he was the best man this country ever produced. It was
quite a while I thought very different ; but some time before
the murder, that's the way I have seen it.".......There was
deep earnestness in the soldier. (I found upon further talk
he had known Mr. Lincoln personally, and quite closely,
years before.) He was a veteran ; was now in the fifth year
of his service ; was a cavalry man, and had been in a good
deal of hard fighting.

Two Brothers, one South, one North—May 28-9.—I staid to-
night a long time by the bed-side of a new patient, a young
Baltimorean, aged about 19 years, W. S. P., (2nd Md. Southern,) very feeble, right leg amputated, can't sleep hardly at
all—has taken a great deal of morphine, which, as usual, is
costing more than it comes to. Evidently very intelligent
and well bred—very affectionate—held on to my hand, and
put it by his face, not willing to let me leave. As I was
lingering, soothing him in his pain, he says to me suddenly,
"I hardly think you know who I am—I don't wish to im-
pose upon you—I am a rebel soldier." I said I did not
know that, but it made no difference.......Visiting him daily
for about two weeks after that, while he lived, (death had
mark'd him, and he was quite alone,) I loved him much,
always kiss'd him, and he did me.

In an adjoining Ward I found his brother, an officer of
rank, a Union soldier, a brave and religious man, (Col. Clifton K. Prentiss, Sixth Md. Infantry, Sixth Corps, wounded
in one of the engagements at Petersburgh, April 2—linger'd, suffer'd much, died in Brooklyn, Aug. 20, '65.) It was
in the same battle both were hit. One was a strong Union-
ist, the other Secesh ; both fought on their respective sides,
both badly wounded, and both brought together here after
absence of four years. Each died for his cause.

May 31.—James H. Williams, age 21, 3d Va. Cavalry.—
About as mark'd a case of a strong man brought low by a
complication of diseases, (laryngytis, fever, debility and
diarrhœa,) as I have ever seen—has superb physique, remains
swarthy yet, and flush'd and red with fever—is altogether

flighty—flesh of his great breast and arms tremulous, and
pulse pounding away with treble quickness—lies a good deal
of the time in a partial sleep, but with low muttering and
groans—a sleep in which there is no rest. Powerful as he
is, and so young, he will not be able to stand many more
days of the strain and sapping heat of yesterday and to-day.
His throat is in a bad way, tongue and lips parch'd. When
I ask him how he feels, he is able just to articulate, " I feel
pretty bad yet, old man," and looks at me with his great
bright eyes. Father, John Williams, Millensport, Ohio.

June 9–10.—I have been sitting late to-night by the bed-
side of a wounded Captain, a friend of mine, lying with a
painful fracture of left leg in one of the Hospitals, in a large
Ward partially vacant. The lights were put out, all but a
little candle, far from where I sat. The full moon shone in
through the windows, making long, slanting silvery patches
on the floor. All was still, my friend too was silent, but
could not sleep; so I sat there by him, slowly wafting the
fan, and occupied with the musings that arose out of the
scene, the long shadowy Ward, the beautiful ghostly moonlight on the floor, the white beds, here and there an occu-
pant with huddled form, the bed-clothes thrown off.

The Hospitals have a number of cases of sun-stroke and
exhaustion by heat, from the late Reviews. There are many
such from the Sixth Corps, from the hot parade of day before yesterday. (Some of these shows cost the lives of scores
of men.)

Sunday, *Sep.* 10.—Visited Douglas and Stanton Hospitals.
They are quite full. Many of the cases are bad ones, lingering wounds, and old cases of sickness. There is a more than
usual look of despair on the countenances of many of the
men; hope has left them.......I went through the Wards talking as usual. There are several here from the Confederate
army, whom I had seen in other Hospitals, and they recognized me. Two were in a dying condition.

Calhoun's Real Monument.—In one of the Hospital tents
for special cases, as I sat to-day tending a new amputation,
I heard a couple of neighboring soldiers talking to each
other from their cots. One down with fever, but improv-
ing, had come up belated from Charleston not long before.
The other was what we now call an "old veteran" (*i. e.*, he
was a Connecticut youth, probably of less than the age of
twenty-five years, the four last of which he had spent in active service in the War in all parts of the country.) The
two were chatting of one thing and another. The fever
soldier spoke of John C. Calhoun's monument, which he
had seen, and was describing it. The veteran said: "*I* have
seen Calhoun's monument. *That* you saw is not the real
monument. But I have seen it. It is the desolated, ruined
South; nearly the whole generation of young men between
seventeen and fifty destroyed or maim'd; all the old families

used up—the rich impoverish'd, the plantations cover'd with weeds, the slaves unloos'd and become the masters, and the name of Southerner blacken'd with every shame—all *that* is Calhoun's *real* monument."

October 3.—There are only two Army Hospitals now remaining. I went to the largest of these (Douglas) and spent the afternoon and evening. There are many sad cases, some old wounds, some of incurable sickness, and some of the wounded from the March and April battles before Richmond. ....(Few realize how sharp and bloody those closing battles were. Our men exposed themselves more than usual; press'd ahead, without urging. Then the Southerners fought with extra desperation. Both sides knew that with the successful chasing of the rebel cabal from Richmond, and the occupation of that city by the National troops, the game was up. The dead and wounded were unusually many.......Of the wounded, both our own and the rebel, the last lingering driblets have been brought to Hospital here. I find many rebel wounded here, and have been extra busy to-day 'tending to the worst cases of them with the rest.)

Oct., Nov. and Dec., '65—(*Sundays.*)—Every Sunday of these months visited Harewood Hospital out in the woods, pleasant and recluse, some two and a half or three miles north of the Capitol. The situation is healthy, with broken ground. grassy slopes and patches of oak woods, the trees large and fine. It was one of the most extensive of the Hospitals—but now reduced to four or five partially occupied Wards, the numerous others being entirely vacant. The patients are the leavings of the other Hospitals; many of them very sad cases indeed. In November, this became the last Military Hospital kept up by the Government. all the others being closed. Cases of the worst and most incurable wounds, and obstinate illness, and of poor fellows who have no homes to go to, are found here.

Dec. 10.—(*Sunday.*)—Again spending a good part of the day at Harewood. As I write this, it is about an hour before sundown. I have walk'd out for a few minutes to the edge of the woods to soothe myself with the hour and scene. It is a glorious, warm, golden-sunny, still afternoon. The only noise here is from a crowd of cawing crows, on some trees three hundred yards distant. Clusters of gnats swimming and dancing in the air in all directions. The oak leaves are thick under the bare trees, and give a strong and delicious perfume.......Inside the Wards every thing is gloomy. Death is there. As I enter'd, I was confronted by it, the first thing. A corpse of a poor soldier, just dead, of typhoid fever. The attendants had just straighten'd the limbs, put coppers on the eyes, and were laying it out.

Three Years Summ'd Up.—During my past three years in Hospital, camp or field, I made over 600 visits or tours, and went, as I estimate, among from 80,000 to 100,000 of the wounded and sick, as sustainer of spirit and body in some degree, in time of need. These visits varied from an hour or two, to all day or night; for with dear or critical cases I always watch'd all night. Sometimes I took up my quarters in the Hospital, and slept or watch'd there several nights in succession. Those three years I consider the greatest privilege and satisfaction, (with all their feverish excitements and physical deprivations and lamentable sights,) and, of course, the most profound lesson and reminiscence, of my life. I can say that in my ministerings I comprehended all, whoever came in my way, Northern or Southern, and slighted none. It afforded me, too, the perusal of those subtlest, rarest, divinest volumes of Humanity, laid bare in its inmost recesses, and of actual life and death, better than the finest, most labor'd narratives, histories, poems in the libraries. It arous'd and brought out and decided undream'd-of depths of emotion. It has given me my plainest and most fervent views of the true *ensemble* and extent of The States. While I was with wounded and sick in thousands of cases from the New England States, and from New York, New Jersey, and Pennsylvania, and from Michigan, Wisconsin, Ohio, Indiana, Illinois, and all the Western States, I was with more or less from all the States, North and South, without exception. I was with many from the Border States, especially from Maryland and Virginia, and found, during those lurid years 1862–65, far more Union Southerners, especially Tennesseans, than is supposed. I was with many rebel officers and men among our wounded, and gave them always what I had, and tried to cheer them the same as any. I was among the army teamsters considerably, and, indeed, always found myself drawn to them. Among the black soldiers, wounded or sick, and in the contraband camps, I also took my way whenever in their neighborhood, and did what I could for them.

The Million Dead, too, summ'd up—The Unknown.—The Dead in this War—there they lie, strewing the fields and woods and valleys and battle-fields of the South—Virginia, the Peninsula—Malvern Hill and Fair Oaks—the banks of the Chickahominy—the terraces of Fredericksburgh—Antietam bridge—the grisly ravines of Manassas—the bloody promenade of the Wilderness—the varieties of the *strayed* dead, (the estimate of the War Department is 25,000 National soldiers kill'd in battle and never buried at all, 5,000 drown'd—15,000 inhumed by strangers or on the march in haste, in hitherto unfound localities—2,000 graves cover'd by sand and mud, by Mississippi freshets, 3,000 carried away by caving-in of banks, &c.,)—Gettysburgh, the West, Southwest—Vicksburg—Chattanooga—the trenches of Petersburgh—the numberless battles, camps, Hospitals everywhere

—the crop reap'd by the mighty reapers, Typhoid, Dysentery, Inflammations—and blackest and loathesomest of all, the dead and living burial-pits, the Prison-Pens of Andersonville, Salisbury, Belle-Isle, &c., (not Dante's pictured Hell and all its woes, its degradations, filthy torments, excell'd those Prisons)—the dead, the dead, the dead—*our* dead—or South or North, ours all, (all, all, all, finally dear to me) —or East or West—Atlantic Coast or Mississippi Valley— Some where they crawl'd to die, alone, in bushes, low gulleys, or on the sides of hills—(there, in secluded spots, their skeletons, bleach'd bones, tufts of hair, buttons, fragments of clothing, are occasionally found, yet)—our young men once so handsome and so joyous, taken from us—the son from the mother, the husband from the wife, the dear friend from the dear friend—the clusters of camp graves, in Georgia, the Carolinas, and in Tennessee—the single graves in the woods or by the road-side, (hundreds, thousands, obliterated) —the corpses floated down the rivers, and caught and lodged, (dozens, scores, floated down the Upper Potomac, after the cavalry engagements, the pursuit of Lee, following Gettysburgh)—some lie at the bottom of the sea—the general Million, and the special Cemeteries in almost all the States— the Infinite Dead—(the land entire is saturated, perfumed with their impalpable ashes' exhalation in Nature's chemistry distill'd, and shall be so forever, and every grain of wheat and ear of corn, and every flower that grows, and every breath we draw,)—not only Northern dead leavening Southern soil—thousands, aye many tens of thousands, of Southerners, crumble to-day in Northern earth.

And everywhere among these countless graves—everywhere in the many Soldiers Cemeteries of the Nation, (there are over seventy of them)—as at the time in the vast trenches, the depositaries of slain, Northern and Southern, after the great battles—not only where the scathing trail pass'd those years, but radiating since in all the peaceful quarters of the land—we see, and see, and ages yet may see, on monuments and gravestones, singly or in masses, to thousands or tens of thousands, the significant word

UNKNOWN.

(In some of the Cemeteries nearly *all* the dead are Unknown. At Salisbury, N. C., for instance, the known are only 85, while the Unknown are 12,027, and 11,700 of these are buried in trenches. A National Monument has been put up here, by order of Congress, to mark the spot—but what visible, material monument can ever fittingly commemorate that spot ?)

As I write this conclusion—in the open air, latter part of June, 1875, a delicious forenoon, everything rich and fresh from last night's copious rain—ten years and more have pass'd away since that War, and its wholesale deaths, burials, graves. (*They* make indeed the true Memoranda of the War—mute, subtle, immortal.) From ten years' rain and snow, in their seasons—grass, clover, pine trees, orchards, forests—from all the noiseless miracles of soil and sun and running streams—how peaceful and how beautiful appear to-day even the Battle-Trenches, and the many hundred thousand Cemetery mounds! Even at Anderson-ville, to-day, innocence and a smile. (A late account says, 'The stockade has fallen to decay, is grown upon, and a season more will efface it entirely, except from our hearts and memories. The *dead line*, over which so many brave soldiers pass'd to the freedom of eternity rather than endure the misery of life, can only be traced here and there, for most of the old marks the last ten years have obliterated. The thirty-five wells, which the prisoners dug with cups and spoons, remain just as they were left. And the wonder-ful spring which was discover'd one morning, after a thunder storm, flowing down the hillside, still yields its sweet, pure water as freely now as then. The Cemetery, with its thir-teen thousand graves, is on the slope of a beautiful hill. Over the quiet spot already trees give the cool shade which would have been so gratefully sought by the poor fellows whose lives were ended under the scorching sun.')

And now, to thought of these—on these graves of the dead of the War, as on an altar—to memory of these, or North or South, I close and dedicate my book.

NOTES.

'*Convulsiveness.*'—As I have look'd·over the proof-sheets of the preceding Memoranda, I have once or twice fear'd that my little tract would prove, at best, but a batch of convulsively written reminiscences. Well, be it so. They are but items, parts of the actual distraction, heat, smoke and excitement of those times—of the qualities that then and there took shape. The War itself with the temper of society preceding it, can indeed be best described by that very word, *Convulsiveness.*

Typical Soldiers.—Even the typical soldiers I was personally intimate with, and knew well—it seems to me if I were to make a list of them it would be like a City Directory. Some few only have I mention'd in the foregoing pages —most are dead—a few yet living. There is Reuben Farwell, of Michigan, (little 'Mitch;') Benton H. Wilson, color-bearer, 185th New York; Wm. Stansberry; Manvill Winterstein, Ohio; Bethuel Smith; Capt. Simms, of 51st New York, (kill'd at Petersburg mine explosion,) Capt. Sam. Pooley and Lieut. Fred. McReady, same Reg't. Also, same Reg't., my brother, Geo. W. Whitman—in '61 a young man working in Brooklyn as a carpenter—was not supposed to have any taste for soldiering—but volunteer'd in the ranks at once on the breaking out of the War—continued in active service all through, four years, re-enlisting twice—was promoted, step by step, (several times immediately after battles,) Lieutenant, Captain, Major and Lieut. Colonel—was in the actions at Roanoke, Newbern, 2d Bull Run, Chantilly, South Mountain, Antietam, Fredericksburgh, Vicksburgh, Jackson, the bloody conflicts of the Wilderness, and at Spottsylvania, Cold Harbor, and afterwards around Petersburg. At one of these latter he was taken prisoner, and pass'd four or five months in Secesh military prisons, narrowly escaping with life, from a severe fever, from starvation and half-nakedness in the winter.

[What a history that 51st New York had! Went out early—march'd, fought everywhere—was in storms at sea, nearly wreck'd—storm'd forts—tramp'd hither and yon in Virginia, night and day, summer of '62—afterwards Kentucky and Mississippi—re-enlisted—was in all the engagements and campaigns, as above.]

I strengthen and comfort myself much with the certainty that the capacity for just such Regiments, (hundreds, thousands of them) is inexhaustible in the United States, and that there isn't a County nor a Township in The Republic —nor a street in any City—but could turn out, and, on occasion, *would* turn out, lots of just such *Typical Soldiers*, whenever wanted.

Before I went down to the Field, and among the Hospitals, I had my hours of doubt about These States; but not since. The bulk of the Army, to me, develop'd, transcended, in personal qualities—and, radically, in moral ones— all that the most enthusiastic Democratic-Republican ever fancied, idealized in loftiest dreams. And curious as it may seem, the War, to me, *proved* Humanity, and proved America and the Modern.

(I think I am perfectly well aware of the corruption and wickedness of my lands and days—the general political, business and social shams and shysterisms, everywhere. Heaven knows, I see enough of them—running foul of them continually! But I also see the noblest elements in society—and not in specimens only, but vast, enduring, inexhaustible strata of them—ruggedness, simplicity, courage, love, wit, health, liberty, patriotism—all the virtues, the main bulk, public and private.)

Attack on Fort Sumter, April, 1861.—What ran through the Land, as if by electric nerves, and show'd itself in stupendous and practical action, immediately after the firing on *the Flag* at Fort Sumter—the Nation ('till then incredulous) flush'd in the face, and all its veins fiercely pulsing and pounding —the arm'd volunteers instantaneously springing up everywhere—the tumultuous processions of the regiments—Was it not grand to have lived in such scenes and days, and be absorb'd by them, and unloosen'd to them?

The news of the attack on Sumter was receiv'd in New York city late at night, (13th April, 1861,) and was immediately sent out in extras of the newspapers. I had been to the opera in Fourteenth street that night, and after the performance, was walking down Broadway toward twelve o'clock, on my way to Brooklyn, when I heard in the distance the loud cries of the newsboys, who came presently tearing and yelling up the street, rushing from side to side even more furiously than usual. I bought an extra and cross'd to the Metropolitan Hotel (Niblo's,) where the great lamps were still brightly blazing, and, with a small crowd of others, who gather'd impromptu, read the news, which was evidently authentic. For the benefit of some who had no papers, one of us read the telegram aloud, while all listen'd silently and attentively. No remark was made by any of the crowd, which had increas'd to thirty or forty, but all stood a minute or two, I remember, before they dispers'd. I can almost see them there now, under the lamps at midnight again.

The ensuing three Months—The National Uprising and Volunteering.—I have said in another place that the three Presidentiads preceding 1861 show'd how the weakness and wickedness of rulers are just as eligible here in America under republican, as in Europe under dynastic influences. But what can I say of that prompt and splendid wrestling with Secession-Slavery, the arch enemy personified, the instant he unmistakably show'd his face?......The volcanic upheaval of the Nation, after that firing on the flag at Charleston, proved for certain something which had been previously in great doubt, and at once substantially settled the question of Disunion. In my judgment it will remain as the grandest and most encouraging spectacle yet vouchsafed in any age, old or new, to political progress and Democracy. It was not for what came to the surface merely—though that was important; but what it indicated below, which was of eternal importance......Down in the abysms of New World humanity there had form'd and harden'd a primal hardpan of National Union Will, determin'd and in the majority, refusing to be tamper'd with or argued against, confronting all emergencies, and capable at any time of bursting all surface-bonds, and breaking out like an earthquake. It is indeed the best lesson of the century, or of America, and it is a mighty privilege to have been part of it.......(Two great spectacles, immortal proofs of Democracy, unequall'd in all the history of the past, are furnish'd by this War—one at the beginning, the other at its close. Those are—the general Voluntary Armed Upheaval— and the peaceful and harmonious Disbanding of the Armies, in the summer of 1865.)

Contemptuous National feeling.—Even after the bombardment of Sumter, however, the gravity of the revolt, and the power and will of the Slave States for a strong and continued military resistance to National authority, was not at all realized through the North, except by a few. Nine-tenths of the people of the Free States look'd upon the rebellion, as started in South Carolina, from a feeling one-half of contempt and the other half composed of anger and incredulity. It was not thought it would be join'd in by Virginia, North Carolina or Georgia. A great and cautious National official predicted that it would blow over 'in sixty days,' and folks generally believ'd the prediction. I remember talking about it on a Fulton ferry-boat with the Brooklyn Mayor, who said he only 'hoped the Southern fire-eaters would commit some overt act of resistance, as they would then be at once so effectually squelch'd, we would never hear of Secession again—but he was afraid they never would have the pluck to really do anything.'.......I remember too that a couple of companies of the Thirteenth Brooklyn, who rendezvou'd at the City Armory, and started thence as Thirty Days' Men, were all provided with pieces of rope conspicuously tied to their musket barrels, with which to bring back each man a prisoner from the audacious South, to be led in a noose, on our men's early and triumphal return! [This was indeed the general feeling, and came to the surface. Still, there was a very strong Secession party at the North, as I shall mention in a Note further on.]

Battle of Bull Run, July, 1861.—All this sort of feeling was destin'd to be arrested and cut short and revers'd by a terrible shock—the battle of First Bull Run—certainly, as we now know it, one of the most singular fights on record. (All battles, and their results, are far more matters of accident than is generally thought; but this was throughout a casualty, a chance. Each side supposed it had won, till the last moment. One had in point of fact just the same right to be routed as the other. By a fiction, or series of fictions, the National forces, at the last moment, exploded in a panic, and fled from the field.)

The troops commenced pouring into Washington, over the Long Bridge, at day-light on Monday 22d—day drizzling all through with rain.

The Saturday and Sunday of the battle, (20th, 21st,) had been parch'd and hot to an extreme—the dust, the grime and smoke, in layers, sweated in, follow'd by other layers, again sweated in, absorb'd by those excited souls—their clothes all saturated with the clay-powder filling the air—stirr'd up everywhere on the dry-roads and trodden fields, by the regiments, swarming wagons, artillery, &c.—all the men, with this coating of murk and sweat and Virginia rain—now recoiling back—pouring over the Long Bridge, a horrible march of twenty miles, returning to Washington baffled, humiliated, panic-struck !...... Where are the vaunts, and the proud boasts with which you went forth? Where are your banners, and your bands of music, and your ropes to bring back your prisoners? Well, there isn't a band playing—and there isn't a flag but clings ashamed and lank to its staff.......The sun rises, but shines not. The men appear, at first sparsely and shame-faced enough—then thicker in the streets of Washington—appear in Pennsylvania avenue, and on the steps and basement entrances. They come along in disorderly mobs, some in squads, stragglers, companies. Occasionally, a rare regiment, in perfect order, with its officers (some gaps, dead, the true braves,) marching in silence, with lowering faces, stern, weary to sinking, all black and dirty, but every man with his musket, and stepping alive;—but these are the exceptions.......Sidewalks of Pennsylvania avenue, Fourteenth street, &c., crowded, jamm'd with citizens, darkies, clerks, everybody, lookers-on ; women in the windows, curious expressions from faces, as those swarms of dirt-cover'd return'd soldiers there (will they never end ?) move by; but nothing said, no comments; (half our lookers-on Secesh of the most venomous kind—they say nothing; but the devil snickers in their faces.)

During the forenoon Washington gets motley with the dirt-cover'd soldiers—queer-looking objects, strange eyes and faces, drench'd (the steady rain drizzles on all day) and fearfully worn, hungry, haggard, blister'd in the feet. Good people (but not over-many of them either,) hurry up something for their grub. They put wash-kettles on the fire, for soup, for coffee. They set tables on the side-walks—wagon loads of bread are purchas'd, swiftly cut in stout chunks. Here are two aged ladies, beautiful, the first in the city for culture and charm, they stand with store of eating and drink at an improvised table of rough plank, and give food, and have the store replenish'd from their house every half-hour all that day ; and there in the rain they stand, active, silent, white-hair'd, and give food, though the tears stream down their cheeks, almost without intermission, the whole time.

Amid the deep excitement, crowds and motion, and desperate eagerness, it seems strange to see many, very many, of the soldiers sleeping—in the midst of all, sleeping sound. They drop down anywhere, on the steps of houses, up close by the basements or fences, on the sidewalk, aside on some vacant lot, and deeply sleep. A poor seventeen or eighteen year old boy lies there, on the stoop of a grand house ; he sleeps so calmly, so profoundly ! Some clutch their muskets firmly even in sleep. Some in squads ; comrades, brothers, close together—and on them, as they lay, sulkily drips the rain.

As afternoon pass'd, and evening came, the streets, the bar-rooms, knots everywhere, listeners, questioners, terrible yarns, bugaboo, mask'd batteries, our regiment all cut up, &c.,—stories and story-tellers, windy, bragging, vain centres of street-crowds. Resolution, manliness, seem to have abandon'd Washington. The principal hotel, Willard's, is full of shoulder-straps—thick, crush'd, creeping with shoulder-straps. (I see them, and must have a word with them. There you are, shoulder-straps!—but where are your companies? where are your men? Incompetents! never tell me of chances of battle, of getting stray'd, and the like. I think this is your work, this retreat, after all. Sneak, blow, put on airs there in Willard's sumptuous parlors and bar-rooms, or anywhere—no explanation shall save you. Bull Run is your work ; had you been half or one-tenth worthy your men, this would never have happen'd.)

Meantime, in Washington, among the great persons and their entourage, a mixture of awful consternation, uncertainty, rage, shame, helplessness, and stupefying disappointment! The worst is not only imminent, but already here. In a few hours—perhaps before the next meal—the Secesh generals, with their victorious hordes, will be upon us. The dream of Humanity, the vaunted Union we thought so strong, so impregnable—lo! it is smash'd like a china plate. One bitter, bitter hour—perhaps proud America will never again know such a bitter hour. She must pack and fly—no time to spare. Those white palaces—the dome-crown'd Capitol there on the hill, so stately over the trees—shall they be left—or destroy'd first?.......For it is certain that the talk among the magnates and officers and clerks and officials everywhere, for twenty-four hours in and around Washington, after Bull Run, was loud and undisguised for yielding out and out, and substituting the Southern rule, and Lincoln promptly abdicating and departing. If the Secesh officers and forces had immediately follow'd, and by a bold Napoleonic movement, had enter'd Washington the first day, (or even the second,) they could have had things their own way, and a powerful faction North to back them. One of our returning officers express'd in public that night, amid a swarm of officers and gentlemen in a crowded room, the opinion that it was useless to fight, that the Southerners had made their title clear to their own terms, and that the best course for the National Government to pursue was to desist from any further attempt at stopping them, and admit them again to the lead on the best terms they were willing to grant. Not a voice was rais'd against this judgment amid that large crowd of officers and gentlemen. (The fact is, the hour was one of the three or four of those crises we had during the fluctuations of four years, when human eyes appear'd at least just as likely to see the last breath of the Union as to see it continue.)

But the hour, the day, the night pass'd, and whatever returns, an hour, a day, a night like that can never again return. The President, recovering himself, begins that very night—sternly, rapidly sets about the work of reorganizing his forces, and placing himself in positions for future and greater work. If there were nothing else of Abraham Lincoln for history to stamp him with, it is enough to send him with his wreath to the memory of all future time, that he endured that hour, that day, bitterer than gall—indeed a crucifixion day—that it did not conquer him—that he unflinchingly stemm'd it, and resolv'd to lift himself and the Union out of it.

Then the great New York papers at once appear'd, (commĕncing that very evening, and following it up the next morning, and incessantly through many days afterwards,) with leaders that rang out over the land, with the loudest, most reverberating ring of clearest, wildest bugles, full of encouragement, hope, inspiration, unfaltering defiance. Those magnificent editorials! they never flagg'd for a fortnight. The *Herald* commenced them—I remember the articles well. The *Tribune* was equally cogent and inspiriting—and the *Times, Evening Post,* and other principal papers, were not a whit behind. They came in good time, for they were needed. For in the humiliation of Bull Run, the popular feeling North, from its extreme of superciliousness, recoil'd to the depth of gloom and apprehension.

(Of all the days of the War, there are two especially I can never forget. Those were the day following the news, in New York and Brooklyn, of that first Bull Run defeat, and the day of Abraham Lincoln's death. I was home in Brooklyn on both occasions. The day of the murder we heard the news very early in the morning. Mother prepared breakfast—and other meals afterward—as usual; but not a mouthful was eaten all day by either of us. We each drank half a cup of coffee; that was all. Little was said We got every newspaper morning and evening, and the frequent extras of that period, and pass'd them silently to each other.)

Sherman's Army's Jubilation, 1865—*Its sudden stoppage.*—When Sherman's Armies, (long after they left Atlanta,) were marching through South and North Carolina—after leaving Savannah, the news of Lee's capitulation having been receiv'd—the men never mov'd a mile without from some part of the line sending up continued, inspiriting shouts and cries. At intervals every little while, all day long, sounded out the wild music of those peculiar army cries. They would be commenc'd by one regiment or brigade, immediately taken up by others, and at length whole corps and Armies would join in these wild triumphant choruses. It was one of the characteristic expressions of the western troops, and became a habit, serving as relief and outlet to the men— a vent for their feelings of victory, returning peace, &c. Morning, noon, and afternoon, spontaneous, for occasion, or without occasion, these huge, strange cries, differing from any other, echoing though the open air for many a mile, expressing youth, joy, wildness, irrepressible strength, and the ideas of advance and conquest, sounded along the swamps and uplands of the South, floating to the skies ('There never were men that kept in better spirits, in danger or defeat—what then could they do in victory?'—said one of the 15th Corps to me, afterwards.)

This exuberance continued till the Armies arrived at Raleigh. There the news of the President's murder was receiv'd. Then no more shouts or yells, for a week. All the marching was comparatively muffled. It was very significant—hardly a loud word or laugh in many of the regiments. A hush and silence pervaded all.

Attitude of Foreign Governments toward the U. S. during the War of 1861–'65. —Looking over my scraps, I find I wrote the following during 1864, or the latter part of '63:

The happening to our America, abroad as well as at home, these years, is indeed most strange. The Democratic Republic has paid her to-day the terrible and resplendent compliment of the united wish of all the nations of the world that her Union should be broken, her future cut off, and that she should be compell'd to descend to the level of kingdoms and empires ordinarily great! There is certainly not one government in Europe but is now watching the war in this country, with the ardent prayer that the United States may be effectually split, crippled, and dismember'd by it. There is not one but would help toward that dismemberment, if it dared. I say such is the ardent wish to-day of England and of France, as governments, and of all the nations of Europe, as governments. I think indeed it is to-day the real, heart-felt wish of all the nations of the world, with the single exception of Mexico —Mexico, the only one to whom we have ever really done wrong, and now the only one who prays for us and for our triumph, with genuine prayer.

Is it not indeed strange? America, made up of all, cheerfully from the beginning opening her arms to all, the result and justifier of all, of Britain, Germany, France and Spain—all here—the accepter, the friend, hope, last resource and general house of all—she who has harm'd none, but been bounteous to so many, to millions, the mother of strangers and exiles, all nations— should now I say be paid this dread compliment of general governmental fear and hatred?.......Are we indignant? alarm'd? Do we feel wrong'd? jeopardized? No; help'd, braced, concentrated, rather. We are all too prone to wander from ourselves, to affect Europe, and watch her frowns and smiles. We need this hot lesson of general hatred, and henceforth must never forget it. Never again will we trust the moral sense nor abstract friendliness of a single *government* of the old world.

No good Portrait of Abraham Lincoln.—Probably the reader has seen physiognomies (often old farmers, sea-captains, and such) that, behind their homeliness, or even ugliness, held superior points so subtle, yet so palpable, defying the lines of art, making the real life of their faces almost as impossible to depict as a wild perfume or fruit-taste, or a passionate tone of the living voice..... and such was Lincoln's face, the peculiar color, the lines of it, the eyes, mouth, expression, &c. Of technical *beauty* it had nothing—but to the eye of a great artist it furnished a rare study, a feast and fascination.......The current portraits are all failures—most of them caricatures.

The War, though with two sides, really ONE IDENTITY (*as struggles, furious conflicts of Nature, for final harmony.*)—*The Soil it bred and ripen'd from—the North as responsible for it as the South.*—Of the War of Attempted Secession— the greatest National event of the first Century of the United States, and one among the great events of all Centuries—the main points of its origin, and the *conditions* out of which it arose, are full of lessons, full of warnings yet to the Republic, and always will be. The underlying and principal of those points are yet singularly ignored. The Northern States were really just as responsible for that War, (in its precedents, foundations, instigations,) as the South. Let me try to give my view.

From the age of 21 to 40, (1840–'60,) I was interested in the political movements of the land, not so much as a participant, but as an observer, though a regular voter at the elections. I think I was conversant with the springs of action, and their workings, not only in New York city and Brooklyn, but understood them in the whole country, as I had made leisurely tours through all the Middle States, and partially through the Western and Southern, and down to New Orleans, in which city I resided for some time. (I was there at the conclusion of the Mexican War—saw and talk'd with Gen. Taylor, and the other generals and officers, who were feted and detain'd several days, on their return victorious from that expedition.)

Of course many and very contradictory things, specialties, prejudices, Constitutional views, &c., went to make up the origin of the War—but perhaps the most significant general fact can be best indicated and stated as follows: For twenty-five years previous to the outbreak, the controling 'Democratic' nominating conventions—starting from their primaries in wards or districts, and so expanding to counties, powerful cities, States, and to the great President-Naming Conventions—were getting to represent, and to be composed of, more and more putrid and dangerous materials. Let me give a schedule, or list, of one of these representative Conventions for a long time before, and inclusive of, that which nominated Buchanan. (Remember they had come to be the fountains and tissues of the American body politic, forming, as it were, the whole blood, legislation, office-holding, &c.) One of these Conventions from 1840 to '60 exhibited a spectacle such as could never be seen except in our own age and in These States. The members who composed it were, seven-eighths of them, office-holders, office-seekers, pimps, malignants, conspirators, murderers, fancy-men, custom-house clerks, contractors, kept-editors, spaniels well-train'd to carry and fetch, jobbers, infidels, disunionists, terrorists, mail-riflers, slave-catchers, pushers of slavery, creatures of the President, creatures of would-be Presidents, spies, blowers, electioneerers, bawlers, bribers, compromisers, lobbyers, sponges, ruined sports, expell'd gamblers, policy-backers, monte-dealers, duelists, carriers of conceal'd weapons, deaf men, pimpled men, scarr'd inside with vile disease, gaudy outside with gold chains made from the people's money and harlot's money twisted together; crawling, serpentine men, the lousy combings and born freedom-sellers of the earth. And whence came they? From back-yards and bar-rooms; from out of the custom-houses, marshals' offices, post-offices, and gambling hells; from the President's house, the jail, the station-house; from unnamed by-places where devilish disunion was hatched at midnight; from political hearses, and from the coffins inside, and from the shrouds inside of the coffins; from the tumors and abscesses of the land; from the skeletons and skulls in the vaults of the federal almshouses; and from the running sores of the great cities.......Such, I say, form'd the entire personnel, the atmosphere, nutriment and chyle, of our municipal, State and National Politics—substantially permeating, handling, deciding and wielding everything—legislation, nominations, elections, 'public sentiment' &c.,—while the great masses of the people, farmers, mechanics and traders, were helpless in their gripe. These conditions were mostly prevalent in the North and West, and especially in New York and Philadelphia cities; and the Southern leaders, (bad enough, but of a far higher order,) struck hands and affiliated with, and used them.......Is it strange that a thunder-storm follow'd such morbid and stifling strata?

I say then, that what, as just outlined, heralded and made the ground ready for Secession revolt, ought to be held up, through all the future, as the most instructive lesson in American Political History—the most significant warning and beacon-light to coming generations......I say that the sixteenth, seventeenth and eighteenth terms of the American Presidency have shown that the villainy and shallowness of rulers (back'd by the machinery of great parties) are just as eligible to These States as to any foreign despotism, kingdom, or empire—there is not a bit of difference. History is to record those three Presidentials, and especially the administrations of Fillmore and Buchanan, as so far our topmost warning and shame. Never were publicly display'd more deform'd, mediocre, snivelling, unreliable, false-hearted men! Never were These States so insulted, and attempted to be betray'd! All the main purposes for which the government was establish'd, were openly denied. The perfect equality of slavery with freedom was flauntingly preach'd in the North—nay, the superiority of slavery. The slave trade was proposed to be renew'd. Everywhere frowns and misunderstandings—everywhere exasperations and humiliations.......(The Slavery contest is settled—and the War is over—yet do not those putrid conditions, too many of them, still exist? still result in diseases, fevers, wounds—not of War and Army Hospitals—but the wounds and diseases of Peace?)

Out of those generic influences, mainly in New York, Pennsylvania, Ohio, &c., arose the attempt at disunion. To philosophical examination, the malignant fever of this war shows its embryonic sources, and the original nourishment of its life and growth, in the North. I say Secession, below the surface, originated and was brought to maturity in the Free States. I allude to the score of years preceding 1860. The events of '61 amazed everybody North and South, and burst all prophecies and calculations like bubbles. But even then, and during the whole War, the stern fact remains that (not only did the North put it down, but) *the Secession cause had numerically just as many sympathizers in the Free as in the Rebel States.*

As to slavery, abstractly and practically, (its idea, and the determination to establish and expand it, especially in the new Territories, the future America,) it is too common, I say, to identify it exclusively with the South. In fact down to the opening of the War, the whole country had about an equal hand in it. The North had at least been just as guilty, if not more guilty; and the East and West had. The former Presidents and Congresses had been guilty —the Governors and Legislatures of every Northern State had been guilty, and the Mayors of New York and other northern cities had all been guilty— their hands were all stain'd.

So much for that point, and for the North.......As to the inception and direct instigation of the War, in the South itself, I shall not attempt interiors or complications. Behind all, the idea that it was from a resolute and arrogant determination on the part of the extreme Slaveholders, the Calhounites, to carry the States Rights' portion of the Constitutional Compact to its farthest verge, and Nationalize Slavery, or else disrupt the Union, and found a new Empire, with Slavery for its corner-stone, was and is undoubtedly the true theory. (If successful, this attempt would of course have destroy'd not only our American Republic, in anything like first-class proportions, in itself and its prestige, but for ages at least, the cause of Liberty and Equality everywhere, and would have been the greatest triumph of reaction, and the severest blow to political and every other freedom, possible to conceive. Its worst results would have inured to the Southern States themselves.)

That our National-Democratic experiment, principle, and machinery, could triumphantly sustain such a shock, and that the Constitution could weather it, like a ship a storm, and come out of it as sound and whole as before, is by far the most signal proof yet of the stability of that experiment, Democracy, and of those principles, and that Constitution. But the case is not fully stated at that. It is certain to me that the United States, by virtue of the Secession War and its results, and through that and them only, are now ready to enter, and must certainly enter, upon their genuine career in history, as no more torn and divided in their spinal requisites, but a great Homogeneous Nation, —Free States all—a moral and political unity in variety, such as Nature shows in her grandest physical works, and as much greater than any mere work of Nature, as the moral and political, the work of man, his mind, his soul, are, in their loftiest sense, greater than the merely physical......Out of that War not only has the Nationality of The States escaped from being strangled, but more than any of the rest, and, in my opinion, more than the North itself, the vital heart and breath of the South have escaped as from the pressure of a general nightmare, and are now to enter on a life, development, and active freedom, whose realities are certain in the future, notwithstanding all the Southern vexations and humiliations of the hour—a development which could not possibly have been achiev'd on any less terms, or by any other means than that War, or something equivalent to it. And I predict that the South is yet to outstrip the North.

Then another fact, never hitherto broach'd, Nationally—probably several facts, perhaps paradoxical—needing rectification—(for the whole sense and justice of the War must not be supposed to be confined to the Northern point of view.) Is there not some side from which the Secession cause itself has its justification? Was there ever a great popular movement, or revolt, or revolution, or attempt at revolution, without some solid basis interwoven with it, and supporting it? at least something that could be said in behalf of it?......We are apt to confine our view to the few more glaring and more atrocious Southern features—the arrogance of most of the leading men and politicians—the fearful crime of Slavery itself—But the time will come—perhaps has come—to begin to take a Philosophical view of the whole affair.

Already, as I write this concluding Note to my Memoranda, (Summer, 1875,) a new, maturing generation has swept in, obliterating with oceanic currents the worst reminiscences of the War; and the passage of time has heal'd over at least its deepest scars. Already, the events of 1861-65, and the seasons that immediately preceded, as well as those that closely follow'd them, have lost their direct personal impression, and the living heat and excitement of their own time, and are being marshall'd for casting, or getting ready to be cast, into the cold and bloodless electrotype plates of History. Or, if we admit that the savage temper and wide differences of opinion, and feelings of wrongs, and mutual recriminations, that led to the War, and flamed in its mortal conflagration, may not have yet entirely burnt themselves out, the embers of them are dying embers, and a few more winters and summers, a few more rains and snows, will surely quench their fires, and leave them only as a far off memory. Already the War of Attempted Secession has become a thing of the past.

And now I have myself, in my thought, deliberately come to unite the whole conflict, both sides, the South and North, really into One, and to view it as a struggle going on within One Identity. Like any of Nature's great convulsions, wars going on within herself—not from separated sets of laws and influences, but the same—really, efforts, conflicts, most violent ones, for deeper harmony, freer and larger scope, completer homogeneousness and power.

What is any Nation, after all—and what is a human being—but a struggle between conflicting, paradoxical, opposing elements—and they themselves and their most violent contests, important parts of that One Identity, and of its development?

Results South—Now and Hence.—The present condition of things (1875) in South Carolina, Mississippi, Louisiana, and other parts of the former Slave States—the utter change and overthrow of their whole social, and the greatest coloring feature of their political institutions—a horror and dismay, as of limitless sea and fire, sweeping over them, and substituting the confusion, chaos, and measureless degradation and insult of the present—the black domination, but little above the beasts—viewed as a temporary, deserv'd punishment for their Slavery and Secession sins, may perhaps be admissible; but as a permanency of course is not to be consider'd for a moment. (Did the vast mass of the blacks, in Slavery in the United States, present a terrible and deeply complicated problem through the just ending century? But how if the mass of the blacks in freedom in the U. S. all through the ensuing century, should present a yet more terrible and more deeply complicated problem?)

The conquest of England eight centuries ago, by the Franco-Normans—the obliteration of the old, (in many respects so needing obliteration)—the Domesday Book, and the repartition of the land—the old impedimenta removed, even by blood and ruthless violence, and a new, progressive genesis establish'd, new seeds sown—Time has proved plain enough that, bitter as they were, all these were the most salutary series of revolutions that could possibly have happen'd. Out of them, and by them mainly, have come, out of Albic, Roman and Saxon England—and without them could not have come—not only the England of the 500 years down to the present, and of the present—but These States. Nor, except for that terrible dislocation and overturn, would These States, as they are, exist to-day.

Extricating one's-self from the temporary gaucheries of the hour. can there be anything more certain than the rehabilitated prosperity of the Southern States, all and several, if their growing generations, refusing to be dismay'd by present embarrassments and darkness, accept their position in the Union as an immutable fact, and like the Middle and Western States, " fly the flag of practical industry and business, and adopting the great ideas of America with faith and courage, developing their resources, providing for education, abandoning old fictions, leave the Secession war and its bygones behind, and resolutely draw a curtain over the past"?

I want to see the Southern States, in a better sense than ever, and under the new dispensation, again take a leading part in what is emphatically *their* Nationality as much as anybody's. Soon, soon, it will begin to be realized that out of the War, after all, *they* have gained a more substantial victory than anybody.

Future History of the United States, growing out of the War—(My Speculations.)
Our Nation's ending Century, thus far—even with the great struggle of 1861 -'65—I do not so much call the History of the United States. Rather, our preparation, or preface. As the chief and permanent result of those four years, and the signal triumph of Nationalism at the end of them, we now commence that History of the United States, which, grandly developing, exfoliating, stretching through the future, is yet to be enacted, and is only to be really written hundreds of years hence.

And of the events of that Future—as well as the Present and the Past, or war or peace—have they been, and will they continue to be, (does any one suppose?) a series of *accidents*, depending on either good luck or bad luck, as may chance to turn out? Rather, is there not, behind all, some vast average, sufficiently definite, uniform and unswervable Purpose, in the development of America, (may I not say divine purpose? only all is divine purpose,) which pursues its own will, maybe unconscious of itself—of which the puerilities often called history, are merely crude and temporary emanations, rather than influences or causes? and of which the justification is only to be look'd for in the formulations of centuries to come? (Let us not be deceiv'd by flatulent fleeting notorieties, political, official, literary and other. In any profound, philosophical consideration of our politics, literature, &c., the best-known names of the day and hitherto—the parties, and their oftenest-named leaders—the great newspapers and magazines—the authors and artists, and editors—even the Presidents, Congresses, Governors, &c.—are only so many passing spears or patches of grass on which the cow feeds.)

Is there not such a thing as the Philosophy of American History and Politics? And if so—what is it?.......Wise men say there are two sets of wills to Nations and to persons—one set that acts and works from explainable motives —from teaching, intelligence, judgment, circumstance, caprice, emulation, greed, &c.—and then another set, perhaps deep, hidden, unsuspected, yet often more potent than the first, refusing to be argued with, rising as it were out of abysses, resistlessly urging on speakers, doers, communities, Nations, unwitting to themselves—the poet to his fiercest words—the Race to pursue its loftiest ideal........Indeed the paradox of a Nation's life and career, with all its wondrous contradictions, can probably only be explain'd from these two wills, sometimes conflicting, each operating in its sphere, combining in races or in persons, and producing strangest results.

Let us hope there is, (Indeed, can there be any doubt there is?) this great, unconscious and abysmic second will also, running through the average Nationality and career of America. Let us hope that amid all the dangers and defections of the present, and through all the processes of the conscious will, it alone is the permanent and sovereign force, destined to carry on the New World to fulfil its destinies in the future—to resolutely pursue those destinies, age upon age—to build far, far beyond its past vision, present thought—to form and fashion, and for the general type, Men and Women more noble, more athletic than the world has yet seen—to gradually, firmly blend, from all The States, with all varieties, a friendly, happy, free, religious Nationality—a Nationality not only the richest, most inventive, most productive and materialistic the world has yet known—but compacted indissolubly, and out of whose ample and solid bulk, and giving purpose and finish to it, Conscience, Morals, and all the Spiritual attributes, shall surely rise, like spires above some group of edifices, firm-footed on the earth, yet scaling space and heaven.

No more considering the United States as an incident, or series of incidents, however vast, coming accidentally along the path of Time, and shaped by casual emergencies as they happen to arise, and the mere result of modern improvements, vulgar and lucky, ahead of other nations and times, I would finally plant, as seeds, these thoughts or speculations in the growth of our Republic—that it is the deliberate culmination and result of all the Past—that here too, as in all departments of the Universe, regular laws, (slow and sure in acting, slow and sure in ripening,) have controll'd and govern'd, and will yet control and govern—and that those laws can no more be baffled or steer'd clear of, or vitiated, by chance, or any fortune or opposition, than the laws of winter and summer, or darkness and light.

The old theory of a given country or age, or people, as something isolated and standing by itself—something which only fulfils its luck, eventful or uneventful—or perhaps some meteor, brilliantly flashing on the background or foreground of Time—is indeed no longer advanced among competent minds, as a theory for History—has been supplanted by theories far wider and higher. ....The development of a Nation—of the American Republic, for instance, with all its episodes of peace and war—the events of the past, and the facts of the present—aye, the entire political and intellectual processes of our common race—if beheld from a point of view sufficiently comprehensive, would doubtless exhibit the same regularity of order and exactness, and the same plan of cause and effect, as the crops in the ground, or the rising and setting of the stars.

Great as they are, therefore, and greater far to be, the United States too are but a series of steps in the eternal process of creative thought. And here is to my mind their final justification, and certain perpetuity. There is in that sublime process, in the laws of the Universe—and, above all, in the moral law —something that would make unsatisfactory, and even vain and contemptible, all the triumphs of war, the gains of peace, and the proudest worldly grandeur of all the Nations that have ever existed, or that, (ours included,) now exist, except that we constantly see, through all their worldly career, however struggling and blind and lame, attempts, by all ages, all peoples, according to their development, to reach, to press, to progress on, and farther on, to more and more advanced ideals.

The glory of the Republic of The United States, in my opinion, is to be, that, emerging in the light of the Modern and the splendor of Science, and solidly based on the past, it is to cheerfully range itself, and its politics are henceforth to come, under those universal laws, and embody them, and carry them out to serve them.. .....And as only that individual becomes truly great who understands well that, (while complete in himself in a certain sense,) he is but a part of the divine, eternal scheme, and whose special life and laws are adjusted to move in harmonious relations with the general laws of Nature, and especially with the moral law, the deepest and highest of all, and the last vitality of Man or State—so those Nations, and so the United States, may only become the greatest and the most continuous, by understanding well their harmonious relations with entire Humanity and History, and all their laws and progress, and sublimed with the creative thought of Deity, through all time, past, present and future. Thus will they expand to the amplitude of their destiny, and become splendid illustrations and culminating parts of the Kosmos, and of Civilization.

Are not these—or something like these—the simple, perennial Truths now presented to the Future of the United States, out of all its Past, of war and peace? Has not the time come for working them in the tissue of the coming History and Politics of The States? And, (as gold and silver are cast into small coin,) are not, for their elucidation, entirely new classes of men, uncommitted to the past, fusing The Whole Country, adjusted to its conditions, present and to come, imperatively required, Seaboard and Interior, North and South? and must not such classes begin to arise, and be emblematic of our New Politics and our real Nationality?

Now, and henceforth, and out of the conditions, the results of the War, of all the experiences of the past—demanding to be rigidly construed with reference to the whole Union, not for a week or year, but immense cycles of time, come crowding and gathering in presence of America, like veil'd giants, original, native, larger questions, possibilities, problems, than ever before. To-day, I say, the evolution of The United States, (South, and Atlantic Seaboard, and especially of the Mississippi Valley, and the Pacific slope,) coincident with these thoughts and problems, and their own vitality and amplitude, and winding steadily along through the unseen vistas of the future, affords the greatest moral and political work in all the so-far progress of Humanity. And fortunately, to-day, after the experiments and warnings of a hundred years, we can pause and consider and provide for these problems, under more propitious circumstances, and new and native lights, and precious even if costly experiences—with more political and material advantages to illumine and solve them—than were ever hitherto possess'd by a Nation.

Yes: The summing-up of the tremendous moral and military perturbations of 1861-'65, and their results—and indeed of the entire hundred years of the past of our National experiment, from its inchoate movement down to the present day, (1775-1876)—is, that they all now launch The United States fairly forth, consistently with the entirety of Civilization and Humanity, and in main sort the representative of them, leading the van, leading the fleet of the Modern and Democratic, on the seas and voyages of the Future.

And the real History of the United States—starting from that great convulsive struggle for Unity, triumphantly concluded, and *the South* victorious, after all—is only to be written at the remove of hundreds, perhaps a thousand, years hence.

DEATH OF ABRAHAM LINCOLN

This book belonged
to Walt Whitman &
was used by him in
delivering his lecture
on Lincoln.
Feby 11th 93.

... ...

& knowing Robert ...

... ... & as ...

the hand of Whitman's

... delight to

... this transfer

to speak a word *reverent* as recalle ~~in memory~~ of this event — and around ~~this~~ *it, indeed,* as emblem and centre for the loss of all *the* soldiers — aye and all civilians too — whose death *resulted* from that war.

~~clear on~~
Twenty two

invited

How often since that dark and dripping Saturday—that chilly April day, now ~~six~~ teen years bygone,—my heart has entertained the dream, the wish, to give of Abraham Lincoln's death its own special thought and memorial. Yet now the sought-for opportunity offers, I find my notes incompetent, (why, for truly profound themes, is statement so idle? why does the right phrase never offer?) and the fit tribute I dreamed of waits unprepared as ever. My talk here ~~which~~ is less because of itself or anything in it, and nearly altogether because I feel a desire, apart from any talk, to specify the day, the martyrdom. It is for his, my friends, I have called you together. Oft as the rolling years bring back this hour, let it again however briefly be dwelt upon. For my own part, I hope and intend, till my own dying day, whenever the 14th or 15th of April comes, to annually gather a few friends, and hold its tragic reminiscence. No narrow or sectional reminiscence. It belongs to These States in their entirety—not the North only, but the South—perhaps belongs most tenderly and devoutly to the South, of all; for there, really, this man's birth-stock. There and thence his antecedent stamp. Why should I not say that thence his manliest traits—his universality—his canny, easy ways and words upon the surface—his inflexible determination and courage at heart? Have you ever realized it, my friends, that Lincoln, though grafted on the West, is essentially, in personnel and character, a Southern contribution?

Though by no means proposing to resume the Secession ~~War to-night,~~ *the evening* I would briefly remind you, ~~my friends~~, of the public conditions preceding that contest. For twenty years, and especially during the four or five before the war actually began, the aspect of affairs in the United States, though without the flash of military excitement, presents more than the survey of a battle, or any extended campaign, or series, even of Nature's convulsions. The hot passions of the South—the strange mixture at the North, of inertia, incredulity, and conscious power—the incendiarism of the Abolitionists—the rascality and *grip* of the politicians, unparalleled in any land, any age. To these I must not omit adding the honesty of the essential bulk of the people everywhere—yet with all the seething fury and contradiction of their natures more aroused than the Atlantic's waves in wildest equinox. *What could*

~~In politics, what can~~ be more ominous, (though generally unappreciated then)—what more significant than the Presidentiads of Fillmore and Buchanan? proving conclusively that the weakness and wickedness of elected rulers, backed by our great parties, are just as likely to afflict us here, as in the countries of the old world, under their monarchies, emperors, and aristocracies. In that Old World were everywhere heard underground rumblings, that died out, only to again surely return. While in America the volcano, though civic yet, continued to grow more and more convulsive—more and more stormy and threatening.

~~Who, I say, can ever paint those years? those peace campaigns preceding, and more lurid and terrible than any war?~~

In the height of all this excitement and chaos, hovering on the edge at first, and then merged in its very midst, and destined to play a leading part, appears a strange and awkward figure.

I shall not easily forget the first time I ever saw Abraham Lincoln. It must have been about the 18th or 19th of February, 1861. It was rather a pleasant ~~spring~~ afternoon. in New York city, as he arrived there from the West, to remain a few hours, and then pass on to Washington, to prepare for his inauguration. I saw him in Broadway, near the site of the present Post-office. He came down, I think from Canal street, to stop at the Astor House. The broad spaces, sidewalks, and street in the neighborhood, and for some distance, were crowded with solid masses of people, many thousands. The omnibuses and other vehicles had all been turned off, leaving an unusual hush in that busy part of the city. Presently two or three shabby hack barouches made their way with some difficulty through the crowd, and drew up at the Astor House entrance. A tall figure step'd out of the centre of these barouches, paus'd leisurely on the sidewalk, look'd up at the dark granite walls and looming architecture of the grand old hotel---then, after a relieving stretch of arms and legs, turn'd round for over a minute to slowly and good-humoredly scan the appearance of the vast and silent crowds. There were no speeches---no compliments---no welcome---as far as I could hear, not a word said. Still much anxiety was concealed in that quiet. Cautious persons had fear'd some mark'd insult or indignity to the President-elect--for he possess'd no personal popularity at all in New York city, and very little political. But it was evidently tacitly agreed that if the few political supporters of Mr. Lincoln present would entirely abstain from any demonstration on their side, the immense majority, who were any thing but supporters, would abstain on their side also. The result was a sulky, unbroken silence, such as certainly never before characterised so great a New York crowd.

Almost in the same neighborhood I distinctly remember'd seeing Lafayette on his visit to America in 1825. I had also personally seen and heard how Andrew Jackson, Clay, Webster, Hungarian Kossuth, Filibuster Walker, the Prince of Wales on his visit, and other celebres, native and foreign, had been welcom'd there, at various times--all that indescribable human roar and magnetism, unlike any other sound in the universe---the glad exulting thunder-shouts of countless unloos'd throats of men! But on this occasion, not a voice--welcoming not a sound.

From the top of an omnibus, (driven up one side, close by, and block'd by the curbstone and the crowds,) I had, I say, a capital view of it all, and especially of Mr. Lincoln, his look and gait—his perfect composure and coolness---his unusual and uncouth height, his dress of complete black, stovepipe hat push'd back on the head, his dark-brown complexion, seam'd and wrinkled yet canny-looking face, his black, bushy head of hair, disproportionately long neck, and his hands held behind as he stood observing the people. He look'd with curiosity upon that immense sea of faces, and the sea of faces return'd the look with similar curiosity. In both there was a dash of comedy, almost farce, such as Shakspere puts in his blackest tragedies. The crowd that hemm'd around consisted I should think of thirty to forty thousand men, not a single one his personal friend---while I have no doubt, (so frenzied were the ferments of the time,) many an assassin's knife and pistol lurked in hip or breast pocket there, ready, soon as break and riot came.

But no break or riot came. The tall figure gave another relieving stretch or two of arms and legs; then with moderate pace, and accompanied by a few unknown looking persons, ascended the portico-steps of the Astor House, disappeared through its broad entrance—and the dumb-show ended.

I saw Abraham Lincoln often the four or five years following that date. He changed rapidly and much during his Presidency —but this scene and him in it, are indelibly stamped upon my recollection. As I sat on the top of my omnibus, and had a good view of him, the thought, dim and inchoate then, has since come out clear enough, that *perhaps* four sorts of genius—four mighty and primal hands, will be needed to the complete limning of this man's future portrait—the eyes and brains and finger-touch of Plutarch and Eschylus and Michel Angelo, assisted by Rabelais.

And now—(Mr. Lincoln passing on from this scene to Washington, where he was inaugurated, amid armed cavalry, and sharpshooters at every point—the first instance of the kind in our history—and I hope it will be the last)—Now the rapid succession of well-known events, (too well known—I believe, these days, we almost hate to hear them mentioned)—the National Flag fired on at Sumpter—the uprising of the North in paroxysms of astonishment and rage—the chaos of divided councils—the call for troops—the first Bull Run—the stunning cast-down, shock, and dismay of the North—And so in full flood the Secession War.—Four years of lurid, bleeding, murky, murderous war. Who paint those years, with all their scenes? —the hard-fought engagements—the defeats, plans, failures— the gloomy hours, days, when our Nationality seem'd hung in pall of doubt, perhaps death—the Mephistophelean sneers of foreign lands and attachés—the dreaded Scylla of European interference, and the Charybdis of the tremendously dangerous latent strata of secession sympathizers throughout the Free States, (far more numerous than is supposed,)—the long marches in summer—the hot sweat, and many a sunstroke, as on the rush to Gettysburg in '63—the night battles in the woods, as under Hooker at Chancellorsville, (a strange episode)—the camps in winter—the military prisons—the Hospitals—(alas! alas! the Hospitals.)

The Secession War? Nay, let me call it the UNION WAR. Though whatever call'd, it is even yet too near us—too vast and too closely overshadowing—its branches unform'd yet, (but certain,) shooting too far into the future—and the most indicative and mightiest of them yet ungrown.

yet

A great literature will arise out of the era of those four years, those scenes—Era compressing centuries of native passion, first-class pictures, tempests of life and death—an inexhaustible mine for the Histories, Drama, Romance, and even Philosophy, of peoples to come—indeed the Verteber of Poetry and Art, (of personal character too,) for all future America—~~for~~ more grand, in my opinion, to the hands capable of it, than Homer's siege of Troy, or the French wars to Shakspere.

But I must leave these speculations, and come to the theme I have assigned and limited myself to.

Of the actual murder of President Lincoln, though so much has been written, probably the facts are yet very indefinite in most persons' minds. I read from my Memoranda, ~~already published,~~ written at the time, on the spot, and revised frequently ~~and finally~~ since.

—The day, April 14, 1865, seems to have been a pleasant one throughout the whole land—the moral atmosphere pleasant too—the long storm, so dark, so fratricidal, full of blood and doubt and gloom, over and ended at last by the sun-rise of such an absolute National victory, and utter break~~ing~~-down of Secession~~ism~~— we almost doubted our own senses! Lee had capitulated beneath the apple-tree of Appomattax. The other armies, the flanges of the revolt, swiftly follow'd.......And could it really be, then? Out of all the affairs of this world of woe and ~~passion, of~~ failure and disorder ~~and dismay~~, was there really come the ~~confirm'd~~, unerring sign of plan, like a shaft of pure light—of rightful rule—of God?.......So the day, as I say, was propitious. Early herbage, early flowers, were out. (I remember where I was stopping at the time, the season being advanced, there were many lilacs in full bloom. By one of those caprices that enter and give tinge to events without being at all a part of them, I find myself always reminded of the great tragedy of that day by the sight and odor of these blossoms. It never fails.)

But I must not dwell on accessories. The deed hastens. The popular afternoon paper of Washington, the little *Evening Star*, had spatter'd all over its third page, divided among the advertisements in a sensational manner in a hundred different places, *The President and his Lady will be at the Theatre this evening.......*(Lincoln was fond of the theatre. I have myself seen him there several times. I remember thinking how funny it was that He, in some respects, the leading actor in the ~~greatest and~~ stormiest drama known to real history's stage, through centuries, should sit there and be so completely interested and absorb'd in those ~~human jack-straws, moving about with their silly little gestures, foreign spirit, and flatulent text.)~~

~~one~~ *imaginary doings.*

On this occasion the theatre was crowded, many ladies in rich and gay costumes, officers in their uniforms, many well known citizens, young folks, the usual clusters of gas-lights, the usual magnetism of so many people, cheerful, with perfumes, music of violins and flutes—(and over all, and saturating all, that vast vague wonder, *Victory*, the Nation's Victory, the triumph of the Union, filling the air, the thought, the sense, with exhilaration more than all per-fumes.)

The President came betimes, and, with his wife, witness'd the play, from the large stage-boxes of the second tier, two thrown into one, and profusely draped with the National flag. The acts and scenes of the piece—one of those sin-gularly written compositions which have at least the merit of giving entire relief to an audience engaged in mental ac-tion or business excitements and cares during the day, as it makes not the slightest call on either the moral, emotional, esthetic, or spiritual nature—a piece, ('Our American Cousin,') in which, among other characters, so call'd, a Yankee, cer-tainly such a one as was never seen, or the least like it ever seen, in North America, is introduced in England, with a varied fol-de-rol of talk, plot, scenery, and such phantasma-goria as goes to make up a modern popular drama—had pro-gress'd through perhaps a couple of its acts, when in the midst of this comedy, or tragedy, or non-such, or whatever it is to be call'd, and to off-set it or finish it out, as if in Nature's and the Great Muse's mockery of those poor mimes, comes interpolated that Scene, not really or exactly to be described at all, (for on the many hundreds who were there it seems to this hour to have left little but a passing blur, a dream, a blotch)—and yet partially to be described as I now proceed to give it...)...There is a scene in the play represent-ing a modern parlor, in which two unprecedented English ladies are inform'd by the unprecedented and impossible Yankee that he is not a man of fortune, and therefore unde-sirable for marriage-catching purposes; after which, the com-ments being finish'd, the dramatic trio make exit, leaving the stage clear for a moment. There was a pause, a hush as it were. At this period came the murder of Abraham Lincoln. Great as that was, with all its manifold train, circling round it, and stretching into the future for many a century, in the politics, history, art, &c., of the New World, in point of fact the main thing, the actual murder, transpired with the quiet and simplicity of any commonest occurrence— the bursting of a bud or pod in the growth of vegetation, for instance. Through the general hum following the stage pause, with the change of positions, &c., came the muffled sound of a pistol shot, which not one hundredth part of the audience heard at the time—and yet a moment's hush—somehow, surely a vague startled thrill—and then, through the ornamented, ~~draperied~~, starr'd and striped space-way of the President's box, a sudden figure, a man raises himself with hands and feet, stands a moment on the railing, leaps below to the stage, (a distance of perhaps fourteen or fifteen feet,) falls out of position, catching his boot-heel in the copious drapery, (the American flag,) falls on one knee, quickly recovers himself, rises as if nothing had happen'd, (he really sprains his ankle, but unfelt then,)—and so the figure, Booth, the murderer, dress'd in plain black broadcloth, bare-headed, with a full ~~head of~~ glossy, raven hair, and his eyes like some mad animal's flashing with light and resolution, yet with a certain ~~strange~~ calmness, holds aloft in one hand a large knife—walks along not much back from the footlights—turns fully toward the audience his face of statuesque beauty, lit by those basilisk eyes, flashing with desperation, perhaps insanity—launches out in a firm and steady voice the words, *Sic semper tyrannis*—and then walks with neither slow nor very rapid pace diagonally across to the back of the stage, and disappears.......(Had not all this terrible scene—making the mimic ones preposterous—had it not all been rehears'd, in blank, by Booth, beforehand?)

A moment's hush, ~~incredulous~~—a scream—the cry of *Murder*—Mrs. Lincoln leaning out of the box, with ashy cheeks and lips, with involuntary cry, pointing 'o the retreating figure, *He has kill'd the President*.......And still a moment's strange, incredulous suspense—and then the deluge!—then that mixture of horror, noises, uncertainty—(the sound, somewhere back, of a horse's hoofs clattering with speed)—the people burst through chairs and railings, and break them up—~~that noise adds to the queerness of the scene~~—there is inextricable confusion and terror—women faint—quite feeble persons fall, and are trampled on—many cries of agony are heard—the broad stage suddenly fills to suffocation with a dense and motley crowd, like some horrible carnival—the audience rush generally upon it—at least the strong men do—the actors and actresses are all there in their play-costumes and painted faces, with mortal fright showing through the rouge, ~~some trembling~~—some in tears—the screams and calls, confused talk—redoubled, trebled—two or three manage to pass up water from the stage to the President's box—others try to clamber up—&c., &c., ~~&c.~~

In the midst of all this, the soldiers of the President's Guard, with others, suddenly drawn to the scene, burst in—(some two hundred altogether)—they storm the house, through all the tiers, especially the upper ones, inflamed with fury, literally charging the audience with fix'd bayonets, muskets and pistols, shouting *Clear out! clear out! you sons of*——.......Such the wild scene, or a suggestion of it rather, inside the play-house ~~that night~~.

Outside, too, in the atmosphere of shock and craze, crowds

and I give it to you, indeed, as a sample: drop of the surrounding ocean.

of people, fill'd with frenzy, ready to seize any outlet for it, come near committing murder several times on innocent individuals. One such case was especially exciting. The infuriated crowd, through some chance, got started against one man, either for words he utter'd, or perhaps without any cause at all, and were proceeding at once to actually hang him on a neighboring lamp post, when he was rescued by a few heroic policemen, who placed him in their midst and fought their way slowly and amid great peril toward the Station House.......It was a fitting episode of the whole affair. The crowd rushing and eddying to and fro—the night, the yells, the pale faces, many frighten'd people trying in vain to extricate themselves—the attack'd man, not yet freed from the jaws of death, looking like a corpse—the silent resolute half-dozen policemen, with no weapons but their little clubs, yet stern and steady through all those eddying swarms—made ~~indeed a fitting~~ the side-scene to the grand tragedy of the murder.......They gain'd the Station House with the protected man, whom they placed in security for the night, and discharged him in the morning.

And in the midst of that ~~night pandemonium of senseless hate~~, infuriated soldiers, the audience and the crowd—the stage, and all its actors and actresses, its paint-pots, spangles, and gas-lights—the life-blood from those veins, the best and sweetest of the land, drips slowly down, and death's ooze already begins its little bubbles on the lips.......Such, hurriedly sketch'd, were the accompaniments of the death of President Lincoln. So suddenly and in murder and horror unsurpass'd he was taken from us. ~~But his death was painless.~~

Thus the visible incidents and surroundings of President Lincoln's murder, as they really occur'd. Thus ended the Attempted Secession of These States. Thus the four years' war. But the main things come subtly and invisibly afterward, perhaps long afterward—neither military, political, nor (great as those are) historical. I say, certain secondary and indirect results, out of ~~the war, and out of the tragedy of~~ this Death, are, in my opinion, greatest. Not the event of the murder itself. Not that Mr. Lincoln strings the principal points and personages of the period, like beads, upon the single string of his career. Not that his idiosyncracy, in its sudden appearance and disappearance, stamps this Republic with a stamp more mark'd and enduring than any yet given by any one man— (more even than Washington's;)—But, join'd with these, the immeasurable value and meaning of that whole tragedy lies, to me, in senses finally dearest to a Nation, (and here all our own)—the imaginative and the artistic senses—the literary and the dramatic ones. Not in any common or low meaning of those terms, but a meaning precious to the race, and to every age. A long and varied series of contradictory events arrives

the true spirit, the true development of
America.

All, all serves. Life serves, &
death also — even the death of th[e]
sweetest and wisest. — Crumbled &
wordless now lie his remains the long buried
in his prairie grave — asi[de]
from cities, and all the din of
wealth-making and politics and a[ll]
contention and doubt. The storm
is long over. The battle, the anguis[h]
the uncertainty whom to trust,
the slur, the envenom'd bullet,
and the sting of many a traitors
tongue and pen part over. With the first
breath of a great historic triumph,
and in murder and horror unsurpassed, Abraham Lincoln died. But
not only the value he gave th[e]
New World in life survives for
ever, but the value of his /
death.

at last at its highest poetic, single, central, pictorial denouement.
The whole involved, baffling, multiform whirl of the Secession
period comes to a head, and is gather'd in one brief flash of light-
ning-illumination——one simple, fierce deed. Its sharp culmination, and as it were solution, of so many bloody and angry
problems, illustrates those climax-moments on the stage of universal Time, where the Historic Muse at one entrance, and the
Tragic Muse at the other, suddenly ringing down the curtain,
close an immense act in the long drama of creative thought, and
give it radiation, tableau, stranger than fiction. Fit radiation——
fit close! How the imagination——how the student loves these
things! America, too, is to have them. For not in all great
deaths, nor far or near——not Cæsar in the Roman Senate-house,
or Napoleon passing away in the wild night-storm at St. Helena——Not Paleologus, falling, desperately fighting, piled over
dozens deep with Grecian corpses—Not calm old Socrates,
drinking the hemlock——outvies that terminus of the Secession
War, in one man's life, here in our midst, in our own time——
that seal of the emancipation of the million slaves——that parturition and delivery of our new-born, at last really free Republic, henceforth to commence its career of genuine homogeneous
Union, compact, untied, consistent with itself.

Nor will ever future American Patriots and Unionists, indifferently over the whole land, or North or South, find a better
seal to their lesson. The final use of the greatest men of a
Nation is after all, not with reference to their deeds in themselves, or their direct bearing on their times or lands. The
final use of a heroic-eminent life—especially of a heroic emi-
nent death—is its indirect filtering into the nation and the
race, and to give, often at many removes, but unerringly, age
after age, color and fibre to the Personalism of the youth and
maturity of that age, and of mankind. Then there is a cement to the whole People, subtler, more underlying, than anything in written Constitution, or courts or armies—namely,
the cement of a death identified thoroughly with that People,
at its head, and for its sake. Strange, (is it not?) that battles,
martyrs, agonies, blood, even assassination, should so condense—
perhaps only really, lastingly condense—a Nationality.

I repeat it—the grand deaths of the race—the dramatic
deaths of every Nationality—are its most important inheritance-
value—in some respects, beyond its literature and art—(as the
hero is beyond his finest portrait, and the battle itself beyond
its choicest song or epic.) Is not here indeed the point underlying all tragedy? the famous pieces of the Grecian Masters—and all Masters? Why, if the old Greeks had had this

THE BRIDE OF GETTYSBURG.

Such was her mother, aye, beautiful 'midst pleasure or despair!
Thank God for this! for this to Him have I prayed both night and day,
Yet to my constant pain and anguish has He kept my child away,

> *[handwritten manuscript overlaid:]*
>
> Thus my friends *(Draw to a)* I finish the
> Duty I spoke of *(and to which I never invited you)* — turning aside
> a moment from all our business
> and pleasure — from the *(rush of)* streets,
> and crowds and din and talk — to
> to give a ~~reverential~~ *commemorative* moment
> this *(twenty fifth)* ~~anniversary~~ to the dead
> President — and in his name, *(and only radiating his spirit)*
> To all the dead soldiers of the
> war — all *indeed* all *(to faithfully fervently invested,)* or lost or won
> *(to say,)* or South, or North,

Her eyes as two stars of light that glad creation with their shine,
Her brow fairer far than Northern snows when nights are cold and long,
Her footsteps lighter than the dews or softest tones of sweetest song.

emotional (eventful)

man, what trilogies of plays—what epics—would have been
made out of him! How the rhapsodes would have recited him!
How quickly that quaint tall form would have entered into the
region where men vitalize gods, and gods divinify men! But
Lincoln, his times, his death—great as any, any age—belong
altogether to our own, and are autochthonic. Sometimes indeed
I think our American days, our own stage—the actors we know
and have shaken hands, or talk'd with—more fateful than any
thing in Eschylus—more heroic than the fighters around Troy:
afford kings of men, (at least for our Democracy) prouder than
Agamemnon—models of character cute and hardy as Ulysses—
deaths more pitiful than Priam's—Afford too, (as all history for
future use is resolv'd into persons,) central figures, illustrators,
in whom our whirling periods shall concentrate—the best future Art and Poetry find themes—and around which the whole
shall turn. #

When, centuries hence, (as it must, in my opinion, be centuries
hence before the Life of These States, or of Democracy, can be
really written and illustrated,) the leading historians and dramatists seek for some personage, some special event, incisive
enough to mark with deepest cut, and mnemonize, this turbulent
Nineteenth Century of ours, (not only These States but all over
the political and social world)—something, perhaps, to close that
gorgeous procession of European Feudalism, with all its pomp
and caste-prejudices, (of whose long train we in America are yet
so inextricably the heirs)—Something to identify with terrible
identification, by far the greatest revolutionary step in the history of The United States, (perhaps the greatest of the world,
our century)—the absolute extirpation and erasure of Slavery
from The States—those historians will seek in vain for any
point to serve more thoroughly their purpose, than Abraham
Lincoln's death.

Dear to the Muse—thrice dear to Nationality—to the whole
human race—Precious to this Union—precious to Democracy—
unspeakably and forever precious—their first great Martyr
Chief.

The last general underpinning
lingering
and result of feudalism

Five loose pages of manuscript inserted in the Reading Book are reproduced on the following pages. They were probably prepared as informal introductory matter in 1887, for the rendition of the lecture at the Unity Church in Camden on April 5 and the one at Madison Square Theatre in New York on the afternoon of April 14.

R. P. B.

my friends

to you this evening

Every subject for my 40 or 50 minutes,

I am not going to

I am not going to
state to you

because I wish to commemorate

and name here with you

the rolling years

* Opt

The central fact of ~~this~~ ^this afternoon^ ~~to night~~ my discourse ~~its~~ ~~predictions~~ will be the death of Abraham Lincoln. An ~~old~~

~~An old~~ Virginia, friend who call'd ^lately^ ~~my house~~ ~~talk~~ ~~pleased~~ ~when the theme of ~~the~~ ~~×~~ ~~being~~ was mention'd, said, "Why rake up the embers of ~~the~~ Secession War? Why the murder of President Lincoln?" adding, "I think we ~~all~~ ^now^ ~~to~~ almost ^hate^ to hear those things mention'd, ^North or south^ let them sleep in quiet in their graves, & mould ^or^ away till gone." — My old friend's suggestion has a certain sound point, which I ^too^ see clearly enough, ^point the^ But I also see ^other^ ~~reasons~~ ~~&~~ surmounting ^and^ enclosing

The war, & the doings
of the war, are facts which
can never be ignored.
But we can treat the
whole matter now and
henceforth. with
even fraternity and
Tolerance and philosophy.

To me, I say, when given
in the true spirit, we can
—neither talk a print can have—
have too many remincscences
of the Secession War and the
and all belonging to it.
things that led to it.

(that period)
(1862 and)

Already, the events of and the years that immediately preceded, as well as those that closely followed them, have quite lost their direct personal impression; and the living heat and excitement of their own time, and are being marshalled for casting, or getting ready to be cast, into the cold and bloodless electrotype plates of History.

Or if we admit that the savage temper and wide differences of opinions and feelings of wrongs, and mutual recriminations, that led to the Secession War and flamed in its mortal conflagration, may not have yet entirely burnt themselves out, still, all will acknowledge that the embers of them are already dying embers, and a few more winters and summers, a few more rains and snows, will surely quench their fires, and leave them only as a far off memory.

Then it has by this time become quite clear to thinking minds,

SOLID LAND APPEARING—THE PEAKS OF THE FUTURE.

But is it not already dawning upon us that out of that War not only has the Nationality of the United States escaped from being strangled, but more than any of the rest, and, in my opinion, more than the North itself, the vital heart and breath of the South have escaped as from the pressure of a general nightmare, and are able to enter on a life, development, and active freedom whose realities are certain in the future, notwithstanding all the Southern vexations and humiliations of the hour; and could not possibly have been achieved on any less terms or by any other means than that war or something equivalent to it. And I predict that the South is yet to outstrip the North.

with the first breath of a great historic triumph & both on murder & horror unsurpassed. Abraham Lincoln himself passed away forever

4

The tragedy itself has
many years been

play

over—and in the peaceful, strong,
exciting, fresh occasions of To-day, and of the Future,
strange, sad war is hurrying even now to be forgotten. The
camp, the drill, the lines of sentries, the prisons, the hospitals,
—(ah! the hospitals!)—all have passed away—all seem now
like a dream. A new race, a young and lusty generation,
already sweeps in with oceanic currents, obliterating that war,
and all its scars, its mounded graves, and all its reminiscences
of hatred, conflict, death. So let it be obliterated. I say the
life of the present and the future makes undeniable demands
upon us each and all, South, North, East, West. .

in every
hateful and
malignant
sense

And now to—

To come back more

definitely to the theme

DEATH OF ABRAHAM LINCOLN

(transcribed from Whitman's reading copy)

How often since that dark and dripping Saturday—that chilly April day, now twenty two years bygone,—my heart has entertained the dream, the wish, to give of Abraham Lincoln's death its own special thought and memorial. Yet now the sought-for opportunity offers, I find my notes incompetent, (why, for truly profound themes, is statement so idle? why does the right phrase never offer?) and the fit tribute I dreamed of waits unprepared as ever. My talk here is less because of itself or anything in it, and nearly altogether because I feel a desire, apart from any talk, to specify the day, the martyrdom. It is for this, my friends, I have invited you—to speak a reverent word as recall'd of this event—and around it indeed, as emblem and centre, for the loss of all the soldiers—aye and all civilians too—whose death resulted from that war. Oft as the rolling years bring back this hour, let it again however briefly be dwelt upon. For my own part, I hope and intend, till my own dying day, whenever the 14th or 15th of April comes, to annually gather a few friends, and hold its tragic reminiscence. No narrow or sectional reminiscence. It belongs to These States in their entirety—not the North only, but the South —perhaps belongs most tenderly and devoutly to the South, of all; for there, really, this man's birth-stock. There and thence his antecedent stamp. Why should I not say that thence his manliest traits—his universality—his canny, easy ways and words upon the surface—his inflexible determination and courage at heart? Have you ever realized it, my friends, that Lincoln, though grafted on the West, is essentially, in personnel and character, a Southern contribution?

And though by no means proposing to resume the Secession struggle this evening, I would briefly remind you, of the public conditions preceding that contest. For twenty years, and especially during the four or five before the war actually began, the aspect of affairs in the United States, though without the flash of military excitement, presents more than the survey of a battle, or any extended campaign, or series, even of Nature's convulsions. The hot passions of the South—the strange mixture at the North, of inertia, incredulity, and conscious power—the incendiarism of the Abolitionists—the rascality and *grip* of the politicians, unparallelled in any land, any age. To these I must not omit adding the honesty of the essential bulk of the people everywhere—yet with all the seething fury and contradiction of their natures more aroused than the Atlantic's waves in wildest equinox.

What could be more ominous, (though generally unappreciated then)—what more significant than the Presidentiads of Fillmore and Buchanan? proving conclusively that the weakness and wickedness of elected rulers, backed by our great parties, are just as likely to afflict us here, as in the countries of the old world, under their monarchies, emperors, and aristocracies. In that Old World were everywhere heard underground rumblings, that died out, only to again surely return. While in America the volcano, though civic yet, continued to grow more and more convulsive—more and more stormy and threatening.

Who, I say, can ever paint those years? those peace campaigns preceding, and more lurid and terrible than any war?

In the height of all this excitement and chaos, hovering on the edge at first, and then merged in its very midst, and destined to play a leading part, appears a strange and awkward figure.

I shall not easily forget the first time I ever saw Abraham Lincoln. It must have been about the 18th or 19th of February, 1861. It was rather a pleasant afternoon, in New York city, as he arrived there from the West, to remain a few hours, and then pass on to Washington, to prepare for his inauguration. I saw him in Broadway, near the site of the present Post-office. He came down, I think from Canal street, to stop at the Astor House. The broad spaces, sidewalks, and street in the neighborhood, and for some distance, were crowded with solid masses of people, many thousands. The omnibuses and other vehicles had all been turned off, leaving an unusual hush in that busy part of the city. Presently two or three shabby hack barouches made their way with some difficulty through the crowd, and drew up at the Astor House entrance. A tall figure step'd out of the centre of these barouches, paus'd leisurely on the sidewalk, look'd up at the granite walls and looming architecture of the grand old hotel—then, after a relieving stretch of arms and legs, turn'd round for over a minute to slowly and good-humoredly scan the appearance of the vast and silent crowds. There were no speeches—no compliments— no welcome—as far as I could hear, not a word said. Cautious persons had fear'd some mark'd insult or indignity to the President-elect—for he possess'd no personal popularity at all in New York city, and very little political. But it was evidently tacitly agreed that if the few political supporters of Mr. Lincoln present would entirely abstain from any demonstration on their side, the immense majority, who were any thing but supporters, would abstain on their side also. The result was a sulky, unbroken silence, such as certainly never before characterised so great a New York crowd.

Almost in the same neighborhood I distinctly remember'd seeing Lafayette on his visit to America in 1825. I had also personally seen and heard how Andrew Jackson, Clay, Webster, Hungarian Kossuth, Filibuster Walker, the Prince of Wales on his visit, and other celebres, native and foreign, had been welcom'd there, at various times—that indescribable human roar and magnetism, unlike any other sound in the universe—the glad exulting thunder-shouts of countless unloos'd throats of men! But on this occasion, not a welcoming voice—not a sound.

From the top of an omnibus, (driven up one side, close by, and block'd by the curbstone and the crowds,) I had, I say, a capital view of it all, and especially of Mr. Lincoln, his look and gait—his perfect composure and coolness—his unusual and uncouth height, his dress of complete black, stovepipe hat push'd back on the head, his dark-brown complexion, seam'd and wrinkled yet canny-looking face, his black, bushy head of hair, disproportionaly long neck, and his hands held behind as he stood observing the people. He look'd with curiosity upon that immense sea of faces, and the sea of faces return'd the look with similar curiosity. In both there was a dash of comedy, almost farce, such as Shakspere puts in his blackest tragedies. The crowd that hemm'd around consisted I should think of thirty to forty thousand men, not a single one his personal friend—while I have no doubt, (so frenzied were the ferments of the time,) many an assassin's knife and pistol lurked in hip or breast pocket there, ready, soon as break and riot came.

But no break or riot came. The tall figure gave another relieving stretch or two of arms and legs; then with moderate pace, and accompanied by a few unknown looking persons, ascended the portico-steps of the Astor House, disappeared through its broad entrance—and the dumb-show ended.

I saw Abraham Lincoln often the four years following that date. He changed much during his Presidency—but this scene and him in it, are indelibly stamped upon my recollection. As I sat on the top of my omnibus, and had a good view of him, the thought, dim and inchoate then, has since come out clear enough, that perhaps four sorts of genius—four mighty and primal hands, will be needed to the complete limning of this man's future portrait—the eyes and brains and finger-touch of Plutarch and Eschylus and Michel Angelo, assisted by Rabelais.

And now—(Mr. Lincoln passing on from this scene to Washington, where he was inaugurated, amid armed cavalry, and sharpshooters at every point—the first instance of the kind in our history—and I hope it will be the last)—Now the rapid succession of well-known events,—the National Flag fired on at Sumpter—the uprising of the North in paroxysms of astonishment and rage—the chaos of divided councils—the call for troops—the first Bull Run—the stunning cast-down, shock, and dismay of Unionism—And so in full flood the Secession War.—Four years of lurid, bleeding, murky, murderous war. Who paint those years, with all their scenes?—the hard-fought engagements—the defeats, plans, failures—the gloomy hours, days, when our Nationality seem'd hung in pall of doubt, perhaps death—the Mephistophelean sneers of foreign lands and attachés—the dreaded Scylla of European interference, and the Charybdis of the tremendously dangerous latent strata of secession sympathizers throughout the Free States, (far more numerous than is supposed,)—the long marches in summer—the hot sweat, and many a sunstroke, as on the rush to Gettysburg in '63—the night battles in the woods, as under Hooker at Chancellorsville, (a strange episode)—the camps in winter—the military prisons—the Hospitals—(alas! alas! the Hospitals.)

The Secession War? Nay, let me call it the Union War.

Though whatever call'd, it is even yet too near us—too vast and too closely overshadowing—its branches unform'd yet, (but certain,) shooting too far into the future—and the most indicative and mightiest of them yet ungrown:

A great literature will yet arise out of the era of those four years, those scenes—Era compressing centuries of native passion, first-class pictures, tempests of life and death—an inexhaustible mine for the Histories, Drama, Romance, and even Philosophy, of people to come—indeed the Verteber of Poetry and Art, (of personal character too,) for all future America—more grand, in my opinion, to the hands capable of it, than Homer's siege of Troy, or the French wars to Shakspere.

But I must leave these speculations, and come to the theme I have assigned and limited myself to.

Of the actual murder of President Lincoln, though so much has been written, probably the facts are yet very indefinite in most persons' minds. I read from my Memoranda, mainly written at the time, on the spot, and revised frequently since.

—The day, April 14, 1865, seems to have been a pleasant one throughout the whole land—the moral atmosphere pleasant too—the long storm, so dark, so fratricidal, full of blood and doubt and gloom, over and ended at last by the sun-rise of such an absolute National victory, and utter break-down of Secession—we almost doubted our own senses! Lee had capitulated beneath the apple-tree of Appomattax. The other armies, the flanges of the revolt, swiftly follow'd. . . . . . And could it really be, then? Out of all the affairs of this world of woe and failure and disorder, was there really come the unerring sign of plan, like a shaft of pure light—of rightful rule—of God? . . . . . . So the day, as I say, was propitious. Early herbage, early flowers, were out. (I remember where I was stopping at the time, the season being advanced, there were many lilacs in full bloom. By one of those caprices that enter and give tinge to events without being at all a part of them, I find myself always reminded of the great tragedy of that day by the sight and odor of these blossoms. It never fails.)

But I must not dwell on accessories. The deed hastens. The popular afternoon paper of Washington, the little *Evening Star,* had spatter'd all over its third page, divided among the advertisements in a sensational manner in a hundred different places, *The President and his Lady will be at the Theatre this evening.* . . . . . . (Lincoln was fond of the theatre. I have myself seen him there several times. I remember thinking how funny it was that He, in some respects, the leading actor in the stormiest drama known to real history's stage, through centuries, should sit there and be so completely interested and absorb'd in those imaginary doings.

On this occasion the theatre was crowded, many ladies in rich and gay costumes, officers in their uniforms, many well known citizens, young folks, the usual clusters of gas-lights, the usual magnetism of so many people, cheerful, with perfumes, music of violins and flutes—(and over all, and saturating all, that vast vague yet realistic wonder, *Victory,* the Nation's Victory, the triumph of the Union, filling the air, the thought, the sense, with exhilaration more than all music and perfumes.)

The President came betimes, and, with his wife, witness'd the play, from the large stage-boxes of the second tier, two thrown into one, and profusely draped with the National flag. The acts and scenes of the piece—one of those singularly written compositions which have at least the merit of giving entire relief to an audience engaged in mental action or business excitements and cares during the day, as it makes not the slightest call on either the moral, emotional, esthetic, or spiritual nature—a piece, ('Our American Cousin,') in which, among other characters, so call'd, a Yankee, certainly such a one as was never seen, or the least like it ever seen, in North America, is introduced in England, with a varied fol-de-rol of talk, plot, scenery, and such

phantasmagoria as goes to make up a modern popular
drama—had progress'd through perhaps a couple of its
acts, when in the midst of this comedy, or tragedy, or non-
such, or whatever it is to be call'd, and to off-set it or finish
it out, as if in Nature's and the Great Muse's mockery of
those poor mimes, comes interpolated that Scene, not really
or exactly to be described at all, (for on the many hundreds
who were there it seems to this hour to have left little but
a passing blur, a dream, a blotch)—and yet partially to be
described as I now proceed to give it. . .

There is a scene in the play representing a modern parlor,
in which two English ladies are inform'd by the unprecedented and impossible Yankee that he is not a man of
fortune, and therefore undesirable for marriage-catching
purposes; after which, the comments being finish'd, the dramatic trio make exit, leaving the stage clear for a moment.
At this period came the murder of Abraham Lincoln. Great
as that was, with all its manifold train, circling round it,
and stretching into the future for many a century, in the
politics, history, art, &c., of the New World, in point of fact
the main thing, the actual murder, transpired with the quiet
and simplicity of any commonest occurrence—the bursting
of a bud or pod in the growth of vegetation, for instance.
Through the general hum following the stage pause, with
the change of positions, came the muffled sound of a pistol
shot, which not one hundredth part of the audience heard
at the time—and yet a moment's hush—somehow, surely a
vague startled thrill—and then, through the ornamented,
starr'd and striped space-way of the President's box, a sudden figure, a man raises himself with hands and feet, stands
a moment on the railing, leaps below to the stage, (a distance of perhaps fourteen or fifteen feet,) falls out of position, catching his boot-heel in the copious drapery, (the
American flag,) falls on one knee, quickly recovers himself,
rises as if nothing had happen'd, (he really sprains his
ankle, but unfelt then,)—and so the figure, Booth, the murderer, dress'd in plain black broadcloth, bare-headed, with

full glossy, raven hair, and his eyes like some mad animal's flashing with light and resolution, yet with a certain calmness, holds aloft in one hand a large knife—walks along not much back from the footlights—turns fully toward the audience his face of statuesque beauty, lit by those basilisk eyes, flashing with desperation, perhaps insanity—launches out in a firm and steady voice the words, *Sic semper tyrannis*—and then walks with neither slow nor very rapid pace diagonally across to the back of the stage, and disappears. . . . . . . (Had not all this terrible scene—making the mimic ones preposterous—had it not all been rehears'd, in blank, by Booth, beforehand?)

A moment's hush,—a scream—the cry of *Murder*—Mrs. Lincoln leaning out of the box, with ashy cheeks and lips, with involuntary cry, pointing to the retreating figure, *He has kill'd the President*. . . . . . And still a moment's strange, incredulous suspense—and then the deluge!—then that mixture of horror, noises, uncertainty—(the sound, somewhere back, of a horse's hoofs clattering with speed)— the people burst through chairs and railings, and break them up—there is inextricable confusion and terror— women faint—quite feeble persons fall, and are trampled on—many cries of agony are heard—the broad stage suddenly fills to suffocation with a dense and motley crowd, like some horrible carnival—the audience rush generally upon it—at least the strong men do—the actors and actresses are all there in their play-costumes and painted faces, with mortal fright showing through the rouge—the screams and calls, confused talk—redoubled, trebled—two or three manage to pass up water from the stage to the President's box—others try to clamber up—&c., &c.

In the midst of all this, the soldiers of the President's Guard, with others, suddenly drawn to the scene, burst in —(some two hundred altogether)—they storm the house, through all the tiers, especially the upper ones, inflamed with fury, literally charging the audience with fix'd bayonets, muskets and pistols, shouting *Clear out! clear out!*

you sons of——. . . . . . . Such the wild scene, or a suggestion of it rather, inside the play-house that night.

Outside, too, in the atmosphere of shock and craze, crowds of people, fill'd with frenzy, ready to seize any outlet for it, come near committing murder several times on innocent individuals. One such case was especially exciting. The infuriated crowd, through some chance, got started against one man, either for words he utter'd, or perhaps without any cause at all, and were proceeding at once to actually hang him on a neighboring lamp post, when he was rescued by a few heroic policemen, who placed him in their midst and fought their way slowly and amid great peril toward the Station House. . . . . . . It was a fitting episode of the whole affair and I give it to you, indeed, as a sample-drop of the surrounding ocean. The crowd rushing and eddying to and fro—the night, the yells, the pale faces, many frighten'd people trying in vain to extricate themselves—the attack'd man, not yet freed from the jaws of death, looking like a corpse—the silent resolute half-dozen policemen, with no weapons but their little clubs, yet stern and steady through all those eddying swarms—made this side-scene to the grand tragedy of the murder. . . . . . . They gain'd the Station House with the protected man, whom they placed in security for the night, and discharged him in the morning.

And in the midst of that pandemonium, infuriated soldiers, the audience and the crowd—the stage, and all its actors and actresses, its paint-pots, spangles, and gas-lights—the life-blood from those veins, the best and sweetest of the land, drips slowly down, and death's ooze already begins its little bubbles on the lips. . . . . . Such, hurriedly sketch'd, were the accompaniments of the death of President Lincoln. So suddenly and in murder and horror unsurpass'd he was taken from us.

Thus the visible incidents and surroundings of President Lincoln's murder, as they really occur'd. Thus ended the Attempted Secession of These States. Thus the four years'

war. But the main things come subtly and invisibly afterward, perhaps long afterward—neither military, political,
nor (great as those are) historical. I say, certain secondary
and indirect results, out of this Death, are, in my opinion,
greatest. Not the event of the murder itself. Not that Mr.
Lincoln strung the principal points and personages of the
period, like beads, upon the single string of his career. Not
that his idiosyncracy, in its sudden appearance and disappearance, stamps this Republic with a stamp more mark'd
and enduring than any yet given by any one man—(more
even than Washington's;)—But, join'd with these, the immeasurable value and meaning of that whole tragedy lies,
to me, in senses finally dearest to a Nation, (and here all
our own)—the permeating imaginative and the artistic
senses—the literary and the dramatic ones. Not in any common or low meaning of those terms, but a meaning precious
to the race, and to every age. A long and varied series of
contradictory events arrives at last at its highest poetic, single, central, pictorial denouement. The whole involved, baffling, multiform whirl of the Secession period comes to a
head, and is gather'd in one brief flash of lightning-illumi-
nation—one simple, fierce deed. Its sharp culmination, and
as it were solution, of so many bloody and angry problems,
illustrates those climax-moments on the stage of universal
Time, where the Historic Muse at one entrance, and the
Tragic Muse at the other, suddenly ringing down the curtain, close an immense act in the long drama of creative
thought, and give it radiation, tableau, stranger than fiction.
Fit radiation—fit close! How the imagination—how the student loves these things! America, too, is to have them. For
not in all great deaths—not Cæsar in the Roman Senate-
house, or Napoleon passing away in the wild night-storm at
St. Helena—Not Paleologus, falling, desperately fighting,
piled over dozens deep with Grecian corpses—Not calm old
Socrates, drinking the hemlock—outvies that terminus of
the Secession War, in one man's life, here in our midst, in
our own time—that seal of the emancipation of three mil-

lion slaves—that parturition and delivery of our at last really free Republic, henceforth to commence its career of genuine homogeneous Union, compact, born again, consistent with itself.

Nor will ever future American Patriots and Unionists, indifferently over the whole land, or North or South, find a better seal to their lesson. All serves the true spirit, the true development of America. Life serves, and death also—even the death of the sweetest and wisest. Crumbled and wordless now lie his remains long buried there in his prairie-grave—aside from cities, and all the din of wealth-making and politics and all contention and doubt. The storm is long over. The battle, the anguish, the uncertainty whom to trust, are over, the slur, the envenom'd bullet and the slug of many a traitor's tongue and pen, are over. With the first breath of a [the?] great historic triumph, and in murder and horror unsurpassed, Abraham Lincoln died. But not only the incalculable value he gave the New World in life survives for ever, but the incalculable value of his death survives forever. The final use of the greatest men of a Nation is not with reference to their deeds in themselves, or their direct bearing on their times or lands. The final use of a heroic-eminent life—especially of a heroic-eminent death— is its indirect filtering into the nation and the race, and to give, often at many removes, but unerringly, color and fibre to the Personalism of the youth and maturity of that age, and all ages, of mankind. Then there is a cement to the whole People, subtler, more underlying, than any thing in written Constitution, or courts or armies—namely, the cement of a first-class tragic incident thoroughly identified with that People, at its head, and for its sake. Strange, (is it not?) that battles, martyrs, blood, even assassination, should so condense—perhaps only really, lastingly condense —a Nationality.

I repeat it—the grand deaths of the race—the dramatic deaths of every Nationality—are its most important inheritance-value—in some respects, beyond its literature

and art—(as the hero is beyond his finest portrait, and
the battle itself beyond its choicest song or epic.) Is not
here indeed the point underlying all tragedy? the famous
pieces of the Grecian Masters—and all Masters? Why,
if the old Greeks had had this man, what trilogies of plays
—what epics—would have been made out of him! How the
rhapsodes would have recited him! How quickly that quaint
tall form would have entered into the region where men
vitalize gods, and gods divinify men! But Lincoln, his
times, his death—great, emotional, eventful, as any, any age
—belong altogether to our own, and are autochthonic.
Sometimes indeed I think our American days, our own stage
—the actors we know and have shaken hands, or talk'd with
—more fateful than any thing in Eschylus—more heroic
than the fighters around Troy: afford kings of men,
prouder than Agamemnon—models of character cute and
hardy as Ulysses—deaths more pitiful than Priam's—Afford too, (as all history for future use is resolv'd into persons,) central figures, illustrators, in whom our whirling
periods shall concentrate—the best future Art and Poetry
find themes—and around which the whole congeries of time
shall turn.

Thus my friends I draw to a finish the duty I spoke of
and to which I have invited you—turning aside a moment
from all our business and pleasure—from the rush of
streets and crowds and din and talk—to give a commemora-
tive moment, this twenty-fifth anniversary to the dead
President—and in his name, and truly radiating his spirit,
to all the dead soldiers of the war—all indeed all—I feel myself to say, to faithfully fervently invested, or lost or won,
or South, or North.

When, centuries hence, (as it must, in my opinion, be centuries hence before the Life of These States, or of Democracy, can be really written and illustrated,) the historians
and dramatists seek for some special event, incisive enough
to mark with deepest cut, and mnemonize, this turbulent

Nineteenth Century of ours, (not only These States but all over the political and social world)—something, perhaps, to close that gorgeous procession of European Feudalism, with all its pomp and caste-prejudices, (of whose long train we in America are yet so inextricably the heirs)— Something to identify with terrible identification, by far the greatest revolutionary step in the history of The United States, (perhaps the greatest of the world, our century)— the absolute extirpation and erasure of Slavery the last, general underpinning and lingering result of feudalism from The States—those historians will seek in vain for any point to serve more thoroughly their purpose, than Abraham Lincoln's death.

Dear to the Muse—thrice dear to Nationality—to the whole human race—Precious to this Union—precious to Democracy—unspeakably and forever precious—their first great Martyr Chief.